Diving & Snorkeling

Thailand

Mark Strickland

John Williams

LONELY PLANET PUBLICATIONS
Melbourne • Oakland • London • Paris

Diving & Snorkeling Thailand
- A Lonely Planet Pisces Book

1st Edition – October 2000

Published by
Lonely Planet Publications
192 Burwood Road, Hawthorn, Victoria 3122, Australia

Other offices
150 Linden Street, Oakland, California 94607, USA
10a Spring Place, London NW5 3BH, UK
1 rue du Dahomey, 75011 Paris, France

Photographs
by photographers as indicated

Front cover photograph, by Mark Strickland
Diver examines soft corals growing on a gorgonian
    skeleton, Similan Islands

Back cover photographs, by Mark Strickland
Porcelain crab on anemone host
Double table coral at Rainbow Reef, Burma Banks
Ornately decorated buddhist temple, Wat Chalong,
    in Phuket

Many of the images in this guide are available for
    licensing from Lonely Planet Images
email: lpi@lonelyplanet.com.au

ISBN 1 86450 201 0

text & maps © Lonely Planet
King Cruiser illustration © Pauli Kuusisto
Current Diving illustration by Suzanne Forman and
    Justin Marler
photographs © photographers as indicated 2000
dive site maps are Transverse Mercator projection

LONELY PLANET and the Lonely Planet logo are
trademarks of Lonely Planet Publications Pty Ltd.

Printed by H&Y Printing Ltd., Hong Kong

Contents

Authors

Mark Strickland

Mark has had a close relationship with the sea from an early age. Growing up in Florida, he has worked many years as an ocean lifeguard, a boat captain and a diving instructor. Mark's passion for underwater photography has led him to many of the world's best diving areas throughout the Indo-Pacific and elsewhere. While each of these areas offers something special, many of Mark's favorite dives are in the vicinity of Phuket, Thailand, where he's been based since 1988. Most of each year, Mark can be found on Fantasea Divers' live-aboard dive vessel, where he has served as Cruise Director and Photo Pro since 1990.

An avid marine naturalist, Mark has discovered several new species of nudibranchs, including one that is named for him, *Halgerda stricklandi*. Mark's photos and articles have appeared in dozens of magazines and books around the world. In addition to representation by several stock-photo agencies, Mark operates his own stock-photo library, Oceanic Impressions.

John Williams

John graduated from Brooks Institute of Photography in California with a degree in Undersea Science and Illustration Photography in 1983. He spent the next five years teaching diving and taking photographs in many exotic locations, and settled in Phuket in 1987. He currently owns a dive shop called Siam Dive n' Sail. His energies these days are devoted more toward writing than photography. This is his third guide about diving in Thailand and Burma. He also writes for Southeast Asia-based magazines and newspapers.

From the Authors

A lot of work goes into a guidebook such as this, and without the valuable insight of those with local knowledge of a particular area, this book would not be possible. The authors would like to thank the following individuals for their valuable assistance during the creation of this book: Steve Blumenthal, Maarten Brusselers, Dr. Hansa Chansang, Danny Curran, Jeroen Deknatel, Andy Dowden, Scott Forbes, Mick Hutchfield, Rob Jacobs, Darren Keet, Surasvadee Kraithong, Pauli Kuusisto, Paul Lees, Anne Miller, Jay Monney, Bill O'Leary, Collin Piprell, Niphon Phongsuwan, Claire Ratcliffe, Brian Raven, Morten Solheim, Somboon Somnavat, Michael Spjuth, Hans Tiboel, Bjorn Vang Jensen, Jason Williamson and Simon Yates. Many thanks, as always, to the Tourism Authority of Thailand. Without their valuable support of the diving industry as a whole, the diving in Thailand would not be as spectacular, well organized and safe as it is today.

Mark Strickland would especially like to thank his wife, Suzanne Forman, for her generous help as underwater model, diving consultant, editorial assistant, artist and provider of immense moral support during the "never ending" book project.

John Williams would like to thank his partner Bent Posejpal who was forced to listen (over several beers) to John's ranting and raving and who kindly reviewed the text whenever asked. Thanks also to his wife, Ohn Mukda, for her incredible patience, which only a Thai can possess.

Photography Notes

Underwater, Mark uses Nikonos V cameras with 15mm lenses for most of his wide-angle work, as well as a Nikon F4 camera with 16mm and 20-35mm zoom lenses in an Aquatica housing. For macro and fish portraits, he uses the same Aquatica/F4 housing, with Nikkor 60mm and 105mm macro lenses. Mark exclusively uses Ikelite strobes (200s and 300s for wide-angle, 50s for macro). Mark prefers Fujichrome films for most uses: Velvia for Macro, Sensia/Provia for wide angle, plus an occasional roll of Kodachrome 64.

Contributing Photographers

Most of the photographs in this book were taken by Mark Strickland. Thanks also to John Williams, Jerry Alexander, Ashley Boyd, Kevin Davidson, Mick Elmore, Sarah J.H. Hubbard, Chris Melllor, Richard Nebesky, Richard I'Anson, Doug Perrine, Paul Piaia, Edward Snijders and Bjorn Vang Jensen for their photo contributions.

From the Publisher

This first edition was published in Lonely Planet's U.S. office under direction from Roslyn Bullas, the Pisces Books publishing manager. Sarah Hubbard edited the book with invaluable contibutions from David Lauterborn and Tullan Spitz. Emily Douglas designed the cover and book and Ruth Askevold assisted with layout. Sara Nelson, John Spelman, Herman So, Mary Hageman and Ivy Feibelman created the maps under the supervision of Alex Guilbert. Justin Marler adapted the illustrations. Lindsay Brown reviewed the Marine Life sections for scientific accuracy. Thanks also to Kevin Garvey of Scuba Junction, Mark Horwood of South East Asia Divers, and Graham Froe and Jason Williamson of South East Asia Liveaboards for assisting with the Andaman Island text. Portions of the text were adapted with permission from *Asian Diver ScubaGuide Thailand*, and from Lonely Planet's *Thailand* and *Thailand's Islands & Beaches*.

Pisces Pre-Dive Safety Guidelines

Before embarking on a scuba diving, skin diving or snorkeling trip, carefully consider the following to help ensure a safe and enjoyable experience:

- Possess a current diving certification card from a recognized scuba diving instructional agency (if scuba diving)
- Be sure you are healthy and feel comfortable diving
- Obtain reliable information about physical and environmental conditions at the dive site (e.g., from a reputable local dive operation)
- Be aware of local laws, regulations and etiquette about marine life and environment
- Dive at sites within your experience level; if possible, engage the services of a competent, professionally trained dive instructor or divemaster

Underwater conditions vary significantly from one region, or even site, to another. Seasonal changes can significantly alter site and dive conditions. These differences influence the way divers dress for a dive and what diving techniques they use.

There are special requirements for diving in any area, regardless of location. Before your dive, ask about environmental characteristics that can affect your diving and how trained local divers deal with these considerations.

Warning & Request

Things change—dive site conditions, regulations, topside information. Nothing stays the same for long. Your feedback on this book will be used to help update and improve the next edition. Excerpts from your correspondence may appear in *Planet Talk*, our quarterly newsletter, or *Comet*, our monthly email newsletter. Please let us know if you do not want your letter published or your name acknowledged.

Correspondence can be addressed to:
Lonely Planet Publications
Pisces Books
150 Linden Street
Oakland, CA 94607
email: pisces@lonelyplanet.com

Introduction

RICHARD I'ANSON

For many of us, mere mention of the word Thailand conjures up images of colorful markets, bustling cities, verdant rice paddies and steamy jungles. Certainly, such features exist here in abundance, yet this Southeast Asian kingdom has far more to offer, including spectacular natural scenery, rich culture and friendly people. Still, there is another side of Thailand for visitors to explore: the wealth of fascinating and beautiful marine life residing amid some of the most attractive, colorful coral reefs found anywhere.

Bathed by the waters of two oceans, Thailand is a country intimately connected to the sea. To the west, the warm waters of the Andaman Sea lap against the length of the Thai-Malay peninsula. The Gulf of Thailand, to the south and east, adds its share to the more than 2,700km (1,700 miles) of Thai coastline. Diving takes place in both the Andaman Sea and the Gulf of Thailand, which offer distinct diving conditions and attractions. While this book primarily covers the waters of Thailand, you'll also find information on two regions with great diving potential just "next door," in the neighboring country of Myanmar (formerly Burma). Though the Mergui Archipelago and the Burma Banks are politically separate from

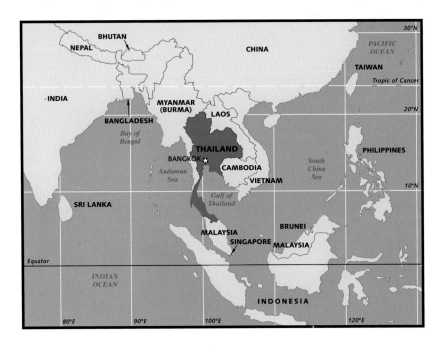

9

Thailand, the regions are a geographic continuation of the islands and reefs of the eastern Andaman Sea. There is also a close affiliation in practical terms since, at least for the time being, the only access to Myanmar's dive sites is by way of Thailand. Additionally, Thailand is one of the main access points for India's Andaman Islands dive sites, which are 800km (450 nautical miles) offshore—they are closer to Phuket than they are to mainland India.

The coral reefs throughout Thailand's waters are home to an impressive diversity of marine life and a wide variety of diving environments. With habitats ranging from shallow coastal areas to remote offshore reefs, both nearshore and pelagic species are found in abundance. Nearly every type of tropical marine life is represented—from tiny nudibranchs to massive whale sharks. Dive site characteristics vary considerably, encompassing coral gardens, rocky outcroppings, steep drop-offs and deep-water pinnacles.

Thailand's infrastructure makes it an easy place to travel, with sea, road or air access to all dive regions. And as Thailand has one of the largest concentrations of dive operators in the Asia-Pacific region, there is seldom a problem finding an available dive boat. With its warm and comfortable climate, well-developed infrastructure and wealth of diving opportunities, Thailand has what it takes to satisfy nearly any diver, whether you are new to the sport or a veteran of dive travel.

This book includes general descriptions of many popular dive sites—as well as some that are not so well known and may be a little more difficult to get to—organized by geographical region. In the Andaman Sea: **Phuket & Neighboring Dive Sites** (including Racha Islands, Ao Phang-Nga, Krabi & Phi Phi Islands); **Trang & Southern Islands; Similan Islands; The Surin Region; Myanmar** (including Mergui Archipelago and Burma Banks); and the **Andaman Islands**. In the Gulf of Thailand: **Western Gulf** (including Ko Samui, Ko Pha-Ngan, Ko Tao and Chumphon) and **Eastern Gulf** (from Pattaya to Ko Chang). Each site is described in terms of outstanding features and typical marine life, as well as depth, currents and other practical considerations.

This book also provides information about the climate, language and culture, entry formalities, getting around, what to bring and more. And since Thailand offers so much more than just diving and snorkeling, you'll also find information on activities to fill your time above water.

JERRY ALEXANDER

Verdant rice paddies are only part of Thailand's draw.

Overview

CHRIS MELLOR

Lying within the tropical northern hemisphere, Thailand stretches more than 1,800km (1,100 miles) from north to south and covers an area of about 517,000 sq km (202,000 sq miles); it is roughly the size of France. Although it shares borders with Myanmar, Laos, Cambodia and Malaysia, Thailand also boasts two extensive coastlines (along the Andaman Sea and the Gulf of Thailand) on both sides of the Thai-Malay Peninsula. Major cities include the northern metropolis of Chiang Mai, Hat Yai in the south, and many other regional centers, as well as the capital of Bangkok. Thailand's population is currently about 61 million, of which about 75% are ethnic Thais. The largest minority group consists of people of Chinese ancestry, followed by Malays and various hill tribes, in addition to numerous other small groups.

History

Buddhist missionaries from India are known to have visited the area now called Thailand as early as the 2nd century BC. By the 6th century AD, a thriving network of agricultural communities existed throughout most of this area. These inhabitants were influenced by many cultures over the centuries. The first true Thai kingdom, Sukhothai, emerged in the 13th century, along with the first Thai writing system. The Sukhothai period is widely considered a golden age in Thai history, when food was plentiful, culture flourished and the kingdom was undefeatable.

By the 14th century, the center of the Siamese kingdom had moved to Ayuthaya and expanded its influence even further, encompassing much of Southeast Asia. Although Ayuthaya fell under Burmese control for a time, the Siamese eventually recaptured their capital. By the early 16th century, Ayuthaya was considered one of the greatest cities in Asia; London was said to be a mere village at the time. The Burmese invaded several times, but the Siamese inevitably regained control. The capitol was relocated to Thonburi, and later moved across the river to its present location in Bangkok.

In the following years, Siam was ruled by a succession of monarchs who further developed international ties, trade and cultural exchange, while avoiding being colonized. In 1932, the king's absolute power was replaced by a constitutional monarchy that is still in effect today. As of this writing, Thailand's King Bhumibol Adulyadej is the world's longest-reigning monarch. The Kingdom of Siam was officially renamed Thailand in 1949.

Geography

Thailand's general shape is said to resemble the head of an elephant, with the relatively slender southern peninsula making up the trunk. Because of its long north-to-south distance (spanning roughly 16 latitudinal degrees), Thailand has perhaps the most diverse climate in Southeast Asia. The topography varies from high mountains in the north to limestone encrusted tropical islands in the south.

The Sunda Shelf extends from the east coast of the Thai-Malay Peninsula to Vietnam, separating the Gulf of Thailand from the South China Sea. The gulf is relatively flat and shallow, with an average depth of 30m (100ft), up to 85m (280ft) at its deepest points. Most of Thailand's major rivers drain into the gulf, tempering the water's surface salinity significantly and reducing nearshore visibility in many places.

On the opposite side of the Thai-Malay peninsula, the much deeper Andaman Sea—more than 100m (350ft) deep in offshore areas—encompasses that part of the Indian Ocean east of India's Andaman and Nicobar Islands.

Almost all diving takes place in the south, among hundreds of islands and reefs found offshore on both sides of the peninsula, not far from the country's roughly 2,700km (1,700 miles) of coastline. Thailand's two principal types of island geography are gently sloped granitic islands, such as those of the Surin and Similan island groups, and the more dramatic limestone islands that characterize marine karst topography, often with steep cliffs, overhangs, and caverns above and below the waterline. Abundant examples of such limestone islands can be found in Ao Phang-Nga.

Dramatic limestone formations are typical of the west coast.

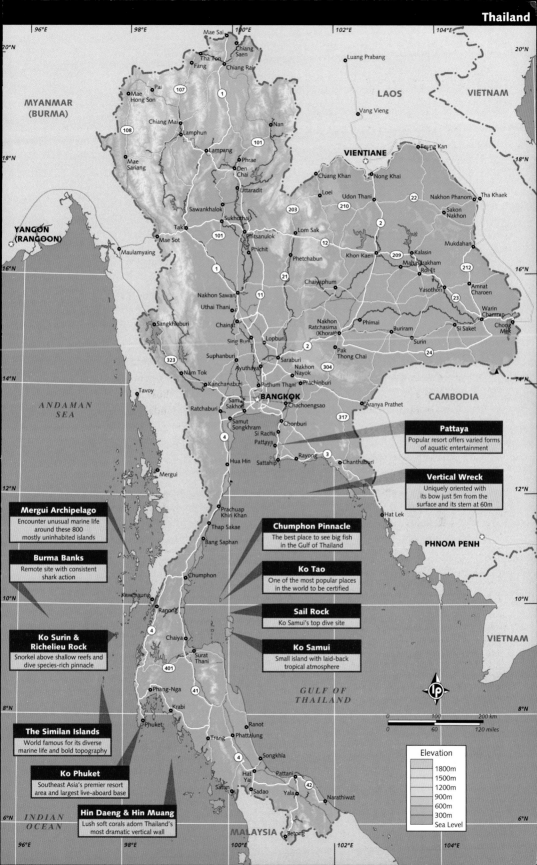

MYANMAR (BURMA)

LAOS

VIETNAM

VIENTIANE

YANGON (RANGOON)

BANGKOK

ANDAMAN SEA

CAMBODIA

Pattaya
Popular resort offers varied forms of aquatic entertainment

Vertical Wreck
Uniquely oriented with its bow just 5m from the surface and its stern at 60m

PHNOM PENH

Mergui Archipelago
Encounter unusual marine life around these 800 mostly uninhabited islands

Burma Banks
Remote site with consistent shark action

Chumphon Pinnacle
The best place to see big fish in the Gulf of Thailand

Ko Tao
One of the most popular places in the world to be certified

Sail Rock
Ko Samui's top dive site

Ko Surin & Richelieu Rock
Snorkel above shallow reefs and dive species-rich pinnacle

Ko Samui
Small island with laid-back tropical atmosphere

VIETNAM

GULF OF THAILAND

The Similan Islands
World famous for its diverse marine life and bold topography

Ko Phuket
Southeast Asia's premier resort area and largest live-aboard base

Hin Daeng & Hin Muang
Lush soft corals adorn Thailand's most dramatic vertical wall

INDIAN OCEAN

MALAYSIA

Elevation
1800m
1500m
1200m
900m
600m
300m
Sea Level

JERRY ALEXANDER

Practicalities

Climate

Most of Thailand's dive regions experience three main seasons: cool, hot and rainy. Though the timing and duration of the seasons may vary from year to year and depend to some extent on the region, there are a few general patterns worth noting.

For most regions, the cool season arrives in conjunction with the northeast monsoon winds, typically beginning in November and continuing through February or March. Sunny skies, balmy breezes and moderate temperatures characterize the cool season. Although evening showers come along now and then, this is the driest time of year.

The hot season falls between monsoons (from mid-March through April). Though warmer and more humid, this period is less windy and seas are often calm.

The rainy season occurs from April or May through October, when the southwest monsoon winds bring moist air from the Indian Ocean. Rain may continue for

General Diving Conditions & Visibility

Though general diving conditions depend on the time of year and location, there is no hard and fast correlation between seasons and visibility, making it hard to predict an optimum date and place to dive. There are a few noteworthy differences between the Andaman Sea and the Gulf of Thailand.

Andaman Sea visibility varies from 5m (16ft) all the way to 45m (150ft) or more. In general, conditions are clearest early in the cool season, beginning in November. Plankton blooms are more frequent in March and April, often causing a noticeable decline in water clarity. During the southwest monsoon (from June through October), visibility can be excellent, although sea conditions often preclude diving at exposed sites. Due to the combination of uncertain weather and unpredictable tourist activity, few Andaman Sea live-aboards operate on a regular schedule from June through mid-October. Daytrips, on the other hand, are available year-round, subject to weather.

In the Gulf of Thailand, visibility is generally not as good as in the Andaman Sea due to freshwater runoff, depth, plankton and water circulation. In general, the northeast monsoon blows vigorously from November through February, hitting the gulf with strong winds that make the seas rough. Visibility also tends to be down, as waves stir up sediment in shallow areas. February through September (at the end of the northeast monsoon and during the southwest monsoon) is generally the best time for diving in the gulf. When northeast winds subside, the seas become calmer and visibility improves. Western gulf sites are relatively protected from strong southwest winds due to their geographical position.

several days at a time, yet extended periods of sunshine and blue skies are common. In fact, many travelers prefer to visit at this time, as crowds are thinner and the overall climate is pleasant.

Although windy weather can occur during both of the monsoon seasons, Southern Thailand rarely experiences typhoons or other major destructive storms. This results in an enjoyable climate throughout the year and also allows for year-round diving.

Water temperature: Sea surface temperatures are generally warm and comfortable. Andaman Sea temperatures range from 26 to 29°C (79 to 84°F). You may encounter chilly thermoclines at depth, especially during March and April. These upwellings are sporadic and seldom last for an entire dive, but may cause water temperatures to temporarily drop as much as 10°C (18°F). Gulf of Thailand temperatures usually range from 27 to 30°C (80 to 86°F) with occasional thermoclines. Temperatures for both bodies of water reach their warmest point during May or June.

Language

The official language is Thai, though several different regional dialects are spoken. English is widely understood around resort areas and by dive operators, but speaking a bit of Thai is appreciated by the locals and will create goodwill. Thai pronunciation is difficult at best, but don't let that keep you from trying to communicate—any attempt is better than none.

Getting There

The majority of Thailand's visitors arrive by air at Bangkok's Don Muang International Airport, which offers direct connections to many of the world's major cities via a variety of airlines. Phuket, Chiang Mai and Hat Yai also have international airports, and while they handle mostly domestic flights, direct international flights are on the increase, especially during high season.

For those already in Southeast Asia, buses from Malaysia make daily runs to Hat Yai, Southern Thailand's main transportation hub. Rail travel from Malaysia and Singapore is also possible and offers good value and a more comfortable ride.

Diving & Flying

Most divers in Thailand arrive by plane. While it's fine to dive soon *after* flying, it's important to remember that your last dive should be completed at least 12 hours (most experts advise 24 hours, particularly after repetitive dives) *before* your flight to minimize the risk of decompression sickness, caused by residual nitrogen in the blood.

Gateway City – Bangkok

Straddling the shores of the Chao Phraya River, the capital is a vibrant, bustling metropolis that is home to some 10 million people. Covering roughly 560 sq km (220 sq miles), the city lies approximately 25km (16 miles) south of Don Muang

PAUL PIAIA
The Chao Phraya River runs through Bangkok.

International Airport, a drive that may take anywhere from 30 minutes to several hours depending on the time of day. Known to Thais as Krung Thep, or "City of Angels," Bangkok has a great deal to offer, provided you are willing to tolerate heavy traffic, polluted air and relentless noise. Boredom is seldom a problem—the city hosts a wealth of cultural attractions, an outstanding variety of restaurants and limitless opportunities for entertainment and shopping.

Getting Around

Thailand's excellent network of domestic flights services most touristed areas. Thai Airways is the main carrier, supplemented by Bangkok Airways and Angel Air. Domestic carriers typically allow less baggage than most international flights; overweight charges can add up quickly. If you encounter such problems, it is worth mentioning that you are a diver, as many airlines allow extra weight for dive gear. If you are planning to visit non-diving destinations in Thailand, baggage storage is available at most major airports.

Bus fares are reasonable and routes extensive, making bus travel a practical mode of transport. The cheapest fares are on the orange government-run buses (*rot tamada*), which tend to make more stops and are therefore slower. The deluxe, air-conditioned "VIP" buses, which service most cities and resort areas, provide a somewhat higher level of comfort.

Compared with buses, rail travel in Thailand is more comfortable and economical, and statistically much safer. About the only disadvantage of the train system is the limited number of routes. You can make advance bookings at Don Muang station, across from Bangkok International Airport. Another option is to book through a travel agent. This generally involves a commission, but can be far simpler than making the booking yourself.

Another good way to get around is by boat; large ferries operate in several areas, namely between Ko Samui, Ko Pha-Ngan and Surat Thani. Ferries also operate between Phuket and Ko Phi Phi, and from Ko Phi Phi to Krabi and Ko Lanta. Smaller passenger vessels are common throughout Thailand, ranging from basic longtail boats to the comfortable, high-speed express boats used in some resort areas.

Other possibilities include rental cars, available in most large tourist centers, and motorcycles, which can be rented even in many smaller towns. Insurance is frequently offered as an option with rental cars; for motorcycles, you're on your own.

Entry

Thailand requires that passports are valid for at least three months from the date of entry. Many foreign nationals (56 nationalities fall into this category) may stay for up to 30 days without a visa, provided they have sufficient funds and tickets for onward travel. A 15-day transit visa is available to 76 other nationalities upon arrival in Bangkok, for a cost of 300 baht. For longer stays (up to 60 days), tourist visas are required.

If you wish to stay longer than planned, you can apply for a one-month extension (600 baht) at any provincial capital's Department of Immigration. Bring one passport photo, as well as two copies of the photo and the visa pages of your passport. Extensions are normally granted only for holders of 60-day tourist visas and those staying on the 30-day no-visa plan. Those with a 15-day visa-on-arrival are not granted extensions unless they hold a passport from a country that has no Thai embassy. Alternatively, visitors may pay a fine (200 baht per day overstayed) at the airport or border when leaving the country, as long as the time overstayed is not excessive (up to 2 weeks or so). Check with any Thai embassy or consulate for further details. Be a little careful of overstays, however, as this is officially against the law, though rarely enforced.

Departure tax is 500 baht (payable in baht only) at international airports. The 30-baht domestic departure airport tax is normally included in the ticket price. However, at the privately owned Ko Samui airport, departure tax varies from 400 to 500 baht, regardless of whether your destination is domestic or international.

Myanmar & India Entry

Thailand is the gateway to Myanmar's Mergui Archipelago and Burma Banks dive sites, as well as India's Andaman Islands. The dive operators will tell you at the time of booking what visa or paperwork—if any—is required. This is the responsibility of the dive operator, but be sure to clarify requirements when you book. At the time of this writing, no visa is required to enter Myanmar (formerly called Burma), but there is an entry fee. A visa is required for entry to the Andaman Islands.

Time

Thailand is seven hours ahead of GMT (London); no adjustment is made for daylight saving time. Accordingly, during standard time, noon in Thailand is 9pm the previous day in San Francisco (PST), midnight of the previous day in New York (EST), 5am the same day in London and 3pm the same day in Sydney.

Money

Legal tender is the Thai baht. Currency exchange offices are common in resort areas; rates are set by the bank and are generally fair and reasonable. Banks and exchanges tend to give better rates than hotels. Major credit cards and traveler's checks are widely accepted.

Local Transportation

Local transportation options vary from one area to the next, but often include taxis, tuk-tuks and baht buses, all of which are taxi-like vehicles with slightly different functions. To further confuse matters, these terms have different regional meanings. Nearly everywhere, a taxi is just what you'd expect—usually some kind of compact car. A

PAUL PIAIA

Local transportion is often both colorful and practical.

tuk-tuk in Bangkok is a small, noisy, three-wheeled vehicle; in Phuket, the same term is used for a four-wheeled mini-bus of sorts. In Pattaya, baht buses are usually small pickup trucks with enclosed passenger areas. Tuk-tuks and baht buses generally operate for a fixed, per-passenger fee (usually about 5 to 20 baht within city limits) and are constantly stopping to pick up or drop off passengers along the way. Taxis generally take passengers nonstop to their destination, with correspondingly higher fares. Most taxis in Bangkok have clearly marked meters: Make sure the meter is on before beginning your journey.

Electricity

The power supply throughout the country is 220 volts, 50 cycles. Outlets may admit either two round pins or two flat, parallel prongs. Standard adapters (available from most travel shops and at airports) are handy to have if you are bringing electric appliances, and a voltage converter may be necessary. Blackouts and power surges are not unusual, so be cautious with equipment without surge protection.

Weights & Measures

The metric system is standard in Thailand, though it is common for Thais to use a mixture of metric and imperial. In this book, both metric and imperial measurements are given, except for specific references within dive site descriptions, which are given in metric units only. See the conversion chart on the inside of the back cover for imperial equivalents.

What to Bring

Topside: Due to the tropical climate, clothing tends to be informal; a few shirts, shorts, a pair of lightweight pants, a long-sleeved shirt, a light jacket or raincoat and, of course, a bathing suit are about all that's needed. Be sure to dress conservatively for visits to religious sanctuaries—shorts and sleeveless shirts are inappropriate for either sex.

Underwater: While many divers prefer to bring their own equipment, rental scuba gear is available through most dive operators. Quality is usually very good, but this is not universally true. In general, reputable and successful operators don't get that way by renting defective equipment; ask around, inspect the gear and stick to well-established dive shops. Tanks and weights are nearly always provided. For snorkelers, bringing gear from home is probably best, since many dive operations don't rent their gear for casual beach excursions, and the snorkel gear provided on general tours tends to be of poor quality. However, these days good quality diving and snorkeling equipment can be purchased for a fair price at almost any seaside resort.

Thermal protection is largely a matter of personal preference. While many divers are comfortable wearing only a lycra skin, a safer bet is to bring at least a 3mm shorty wetsuit, especially if thermoclines are present or if you are diving between November and January. If you are a photographer who spends a lot of time in one place, or you simply hate to be cold, even a 3 or 4mm full wetsuit would not be overdoing it.

As with professional dive centers elsewhere in the world, most operators will require you to show your certification card, and it is never a bad idea to bring your logbook as well. If you plan to get certified in Thailand, bring several passport-sized color photos, which will be used to create your certification card.

Underwater Photography & Video

Most standard films and videotapes are available and reasonably priced, so it's not necessary to bring them. However, if you require specialty items or professional film, it's best to bring them from home. You can rent underwater cameras of varying quality at many dive shops. For those who plan to stay within snorkeling depths, disposable underwater cameras are inexpensive and work pretty well; they are available at many photo shops around resort areas.

Color print processing is available throughout Thailand, and slide film can be developed in most larger cities and resort areas and on some live-aboards. The processing quality for prints is usually fine, but for slides it pays to be more selective. For a better chance of good results, choose a high-volume processing lab—high turnover usually means fresher chemicals. If this is not an option, you may be better off waiting until you get home.

Business Hours

Business hours depend largely on where you are. In tourist areas, many shops don't open until 9am or later, but often stay open well into the evening. In smaller towns, business hours more closely match the sun, with doors opening as early as 7am and closing at 5 or 6pm. Most businesses are open on Saturdays, but many are closed on Sundays. Banks are typically open weekdays from 8am to 3:30pm, while those in tourist areas may have extended hours. Government offices are usually open 8:30am to 4:30pm, but close for lunch from noon to 1pm. Bear in mind that neither banks nor government offices are open on public holidays or weekends (except for exchange banks, which are found in nearly all Thai towns).

Accommodations

A wide range of lodging is available in most areas, from simple, inexpensive bungalows to ultra-luxurious five-star hotels. Rates can run from 300 baht or less for a basic bungalow to 20,000 baht or more for top resorts. Space tends to be limited from Christmas until a few weeks after New Year's, as well as Chinese New Year (February or March) and Songkran (mid-April), so reserve early if you plan to visit at these times. Many hotels charge a peak-season surcharge of 10% to 15% from late December through late January.

Simple accommodations (ranging from small tents to large bungalows) are available at most parks, as are campsites for those who are self-sufficent. Reservations are recommended from mid-December to mid-April. Call the National Parks Division at ☎ (2) 579 4842 or 579 0529 or visit Phahonyothin Road, Bangkhen (north Bangkok). Bookings must be paid in advance.

Dining & Food

Thai people consider eating to be one of life's great pleasures, and meals are typically a feast for the eyes as well as the palate. A typical Thai meal does not consist of only spicy food, but is balanced by several different tastes—usually sour, sweet, salty and spicy. Unfortunately, authentically seasoned food is increasingly hard to find in tourist areas; if you like it hot, emphasize your preference when ordering. (*Pet* is Thai for spicy, *pet mahk* means very spicy and *rop chat khon Thai* means you want it like the locals eat it—not necessarily more spicy, but as it should be prepared according to local Thai traditions.) Most resort areas also offer plenty of international cuisine, and fast-food fare is also well represented.

Tipping is not common in Thailand, though they are getting used to it in tourist hotels and restaurants. Check to see if a "service charge" has been included in the bill. If it has, don't leave a tip. If not, you may tip about 10% of the bill or what you feel is appropriate (there is no standard amount to leave).

Shopping

A wide range of handicrafts and indigenous art is available at shops and markets throughout the country, especially in resort areas. Some of the more authentic choices include finely detailed buffalo-hide carvings, ornately painted lacquerware jars and figurines, intricate woodcarvings and colorful hand-painted batiks. Custom tailored clothes are also an excellent value; workmanship is generally very good and fabric selection is extensive. Gems and jewelry can also be good buys, but unless you are an expert, stick to shops that are approved by the Tourist Authority of Thailand. Though store prices are usually set, bargaining is a common—even expected—part of purchasing something at open-air street stalls.

You are likely to see various "souvenirs from the sea," including shark jaws, dried pufferfish, seahorses, corals and a dazzling array of seashells. While it may be tempting to purchase such items, remember where they come from. Marine life killed needlessly for souvenirs means fewer creatures the next time you go diving.

Activities & Attractions

RICHARD I'ANSON

Thailand boasts an incredible range of things to do and see. Possibilities include a wide spectrum of cultural, historical and natural attractions, outdoor activities and water sports, spectator sporting events and, in some areas, lively entertainment and nightlife.

Cultural & Historical Attractions

For a colorful taste of local culture, be sure to visit a **traditional market**. Typically, a number of vendors congregate outdoors to sell a variety of products, such as produce, seafood, meat, snacks, household goods, clothing, fresh flowers and much more. Small villages normally have a market day every few days; in bigger cities it's a daily event. In any case, the earlier you visit, the more you're likely to see.

Throughout the country, the graceful spires of Buddhist **temples**, or *wats*, reach toward the sky. Aside from serving as spiritual and religious centers, wats sometimes function as schools, clinics and geriatric wards, depending on the needs of the community. Many wats house some of the country's finest examples of traditional sculpture and painting. Of course, every wat also contains at least one Buddha image. Among the most notable of these are the "Emerald" Buddha at Wat Phra Kaew, the 46m (150ft) long reclining Buddha at Wat Pho, and the 3m (10ft) tall, 5½ ton solid-gold Buddha at Wat Traimit, all in Bangkok.

Other interesting examples of Thai architecture include **spirit houses**—finely detailed miniature dwellings built in the traditional Thai style, part of a custom that predates Buddhism. Intended to provide a comfortable abode for any restless spirits that might otherwise inhabit a home or business, these splendid little structures can be found mounted on pedestals in nearly every front yard in Thailand.

The creative energy of the Thais extends beyond the realm of tangible objects to a unique style of **music** and **dance**. Traditional Thai dancers are a study of discipline and grace, their every motion carefully choreographed to tell time-honored legends as they move in harmony with classical Thai music. Dinner-show performances are frequently offered at larger hotels and resorts.

Aside from traditional music and dance, most tourist areas also offer some nighttime entertainment possibilities. **Nightlife** options in bigger towns include coffee shops, cybercafés, mini-golf, pubs, live music and discos, as well as the "hostess" bars and cabarets that Thailand is infamous for. **Movie theaters** are found across the country, although soundtracks are usually dubbed in Thai. English-language films are shown at a few theatres in Bangkok, Pattaya and Phuket. Regardless of the soundtrack, the royal anthem is played before every movie and the audience is expected to stand at this time.

Outdoor Activities

High on Thailand's list of attractions is its magnificent scenery. Outstanding natural features include the north's steep mountains, towering limestone monoliths in the south, numerous caves and rock formations and an extensive network of lakes, rivers, streams, waterfalls and wetlands.

Biodiversity

Bordered by two major bodies of water and spanning more than 1,800km (1,100 miles) from north to south, Thailand encompasses several distinct climatic zones and occupies a unique biological crossroads between equatorial plains and Himalayan foothills. With such a wide range of environments, it is not surprising that biodiversity here is among the greatest in Asia. An extraordinary variety of wildlife exists within the country's natural areas, which are home to some 27,000 species of flowering plants and a comparably diverse animal population, including some of the world's rarest species, such as clouded leopards, dusky langurs and piliated gibbons.

No vacation in Thailand would be complete without visiting at least one **national park**. Fortunately, parks are numerous and widely distributed throughout the country; you shouldn't have to go far out of your way to find one. Most parks charge a modest entry fee—typically 15 to 30 baht for foreigners, considerably less for Thais. For an excellent guide to Thailand's protected areas, pick up a copy of *National Parks of Thailand* (ISBN 974-88670-9-9).

One of northern Thailand's biggest draws is wilderness walking, also called **trekking**. Typical itineraries run from three to five days, although it is possible to arrange a trip of any length. Most treks involve daily hikes through forested mountain areas, coupled with overnight stays in hilltribe villages where the guide doubles as cook and interpreter. While walking is the primary mode of transportation, many treks also give guests a chance to try elephant riding and river rafting somewhere along the route. The least expensive treks usually involve joining a group of six to ten fellow adventurers, but more-exclusive options do exist. Arrangements can be made through most travel agents.

For those who don't have the time or inclination to join a multi-day trek, **elephant trekking** has become a popular alternative. Typical tours take place in forested areas close to tourist centers and last from one hour to half a day, which is about the limit of most people's comfort threshold on the lumbering beasts.

For those who prefer a bit more independence, **hiking** is another way to enjoy Thailand's natural beauty without joining an organized tour. Options range from casual one-hour walks to multi-day excursions for those who have their own gear. Guided hikes—during which, for a reasonable rate, park rangers are hired as guides and cooks—are available in southern Thailand's larger national parks (Kaeng Krachan, Khao Lak, Khao Sam Roi Yot, Khao Sok and Thaleh Ban). Parks with marked trails (suitable for hiking without a guide) include Khao Sam Roi Yot, Khao Sok and Ko Tarutao. Inter-village footpaths on southern Ko Chang can also be hiked without guides, though paths through the island's hilly interior can be challenging due to steep

View Thailand's rainforests from the back of an elephant.

grades and undergrowth. When hiking without a guide, it is recommended that you hike with at least one other person and that you let someone in the local community know where you're headed and for how long. Some of the more popular national parks have trail maps available; inquire at park headquarters.

Sea kayaking is one of the best ways to enjoy the marine environment (other than diving or snorkeling). One of the most popular areas for kayaking is in Ao Phang-Nga, just east of Phuket. Aside from its proximity to this resort island, the main attraction for kayakers is the maze of spectacular limestone islands

Hong Sweet Hong

If seen from the air, the limestone islands of Ao Phang-Nga appear as if some giant dug huge holes from the top all the way down to sea level. Within these holes, called *hong*s in Thai, are shallow mangrove lagoons—hidden, mini-ecosystems that are largely isolated from the outside world. In some cases, horizontal caves connect the vertical hongs to the surrounding water, allowing kayakers to access these unique and fascinating habitats.

While it may be possible to rent sea kayaks for a coastal excursion, the only way to experience the hongs is to join a guided kayak tour. Unfortunately, the surging popularity of this activity has resulted in overcrowding in recent years, especially in high season, detracting considerably from the otherwise pristine atmosphere. To avoid the crowds, consider signing up for a multiple-night trip to one of the more remote areas.

dotting the shallow bay. Jutting skyward like natural skyscrapers, these monoliths are constantly eroded by wave action and rainwater. Consequently, many are riddled with horizontal, sea-level cave systems, as well as vertical, open-air rooms, or *hongs*.

Kayakers explore an island in Ao Phang-Nga.

Sailing opportunities are excellent year-round, with a seemingly endless supply of beautiful, peaceful anchorages on both the east and west coasts. While wind blows amply throughout most of the year, breezes in March and April tend to be light and variable. For experienced sailors who wish to enjoy some snorkeling and sailing without the help of a local crew, a few companies in Thailand—mainly in Phuket—offer bareboat charters (renting a boat without captain or crew).

Spectator Sports

In the martial sport **Muay Thai** (**Thai boxing**), almost anything goes, both in the ring and in the stands. If you don't mind the violence (in the ring), a Thai boxing match is worth attending for the pure spectacle—the wild musical accompaniment, the ceremonial beginning of each match and the frenzied betting around the stadium. As Thai boxing becomes more popular with westerners, more bouts are staged in tourist towns. In these, the action may be genuine but the judging below par. Nonetheless, it is easy to find authentic matches, which are held daily at the major Bangkok stadiums and in the provinces.

Takraw is a more relaxing spectator sport that takes several forms depending on where it is played. In the most popular and international version, a small woven rattan ball is hit over a net separating two teams. The game follows the same rules as volleyball, except players can touch the ball with only their feet and head. It's not necessary to attend a big event to enjoy the sport, however, as many villages have nets where games are held regularly, usually in late afternoon.

Diving Health & Safety

ASHLEY BOYD

Overall, Thailand has quite a high standard of health, and medical treatment is generally fairly good, although access depends very much on your location. While the country's most technologically advanced hospitals are in big cities like Bangkok, Phuket and Hat Yai, every provincial capital has at least one hospital. Even smaller towns usually have a basic clinic or two.

The most important health rule is to be careful about what you eat and drink—stomach upsets are the most common health problem for travelers. Thoroughly cooked food is safest, but it is risky if it has been sitting around for hours before being consumed. Fruit that can be peeled is a safe bet, but salads can be problematic if not washed thoroughly. Drink only bottled, purified water and avoid ice that is not made from purified water. (Bottled water and purified ice are the norm at almost all restaurants, bars and hotels.) Also be sure to drink enough—dehydration can be a big problem in the tropics and is often a contributing factor to decompression sickness.

Malaria is a potentially fatal, mosquito-borne disease found in many tropical areas. In Thailand, it is virtually unknown around most dive resorts and large cities, but if you plan on trekking up north or going ashore in remote areas—including Trat Province and Ko Chang, northern Kanchanaburi Province, Ko Pha-Ngan and Ko Tao, and the Mergui Archipelago—preventive medications are in order. Most preventive treatments need to be started several weeks prior to traveling, so see your medical provider early to discuss options. The best way to avoid malaria is to not get bitten. In malaria-prone regions, wear long pants, socks and long-sleeved shirts and sleep under a mosquito net. Using insect repellent and burning mosquito coils or citronella candles is also helpful. The mosquitoes that cause malaria are active only from dusk to dawn, so these hours merit special caution.

Dengue fever is another mosquito-borne malady, though fortunately it is usually not as dangerous as malaria. There are no preventive drugs for dengue, nor is there any treatment other than lots of rest. Although chances of contracting it in Thailand are not great, the same simple precautions apply. (Unlike malaria, the mosquito that causes dengue is most active in the daytime.)

The U.S. Centers for Disease Control and Prevention regularly posts updates on health-related concerns around the world specifically for travelers. Contact the CDC by fax or visit their website. Call (toll-free from the U.S.) ☎ 888-232-3299 and request Document 000005 to receive a list of documents available by fax. Their website is www.cdc.gov.

Pre-Trip Preparation

At least a month before your trip, inspect your dive gear. Remember, your regulator should be serviced annually, whether you've used it or not. If you use a dive computer and can replace the battery yourself, change it before the trip or buy a spare one to take along. Otherwise, send the computer to the manufacturer for a battery replacement. If possible, find out if the dive center rents or services the type of gear you own. If not, you might want to take spare parts or even spare gear. Purchase any additional equipment you may need, such as a dive light and tank marker light for night diving, a line reel for wreck diving, etc. Make sure you have at least a whistle attached to your BC, and be sure to pack a surface marker tube (also known as a safety sausage, come-to-me or elephant condom).

About a week before your departure, do a final check of your gear, grease o-rings, check batteries and assemble a save-a-dive kit. Don't forget to pack a first-aid kit and medications such as decongestants, ear drops, antihistamines, antibiotic ointment, insect repellent and motion sickness tablets.

While entry into Thailand does not require any vaccinations (unless you're coming from an infected area) it is not a bad idea to take certain precautions. Depending on your planned activities and the areas you wish to visit, recommended vaccinations may include tetanus, diphtheria, typhoid, rabies and hepatitis A and B. Since some vaccines require multiple shots over a period of several months, it's best to visit a doctor well prior to setting off.

Signaling Devices

SARAH J. H. HUBBARD

One of the greatest dangers of open-water diving is the possibility of drifting away at the surface without being seen. Make sure this never happens to you! A diver is extremely difficult to locate in the water, so always dive with a signaling device of some sort, preferably more than one.

One good signaling device that is also the easiest to carry is a whistle—even the little ones are quite effective. Use a zip tie to attach one permanently to your BC. Even better, though more expensive, is a loud horn that connects to the inflator hose. To operate it, simply push a button to let out a blast. It does require air from your tank to function, though.

It is imperative that you can be seen as well as heard. One of the most important pieces of dive equipment to carry is a marker tube, pictured here. The best ones are bright in color and about 3m (10ft) long. They roll up and will easily fit into a BC pocket or clip onto a D-ring. They are inflated orally or with a regulator. Some allow you to insert a dive light into the tube—a nice feature when it is dark.

Other signaling aides include mirrors, flares and dye markers, but these have limited reliability. A simple dive light is particularly versatile. Not only can it be used during the day for looking into crevices and crannies, but it also comes in handy for nighttime signaling.

Recompression Facilities

While Thailand has four working recompression chambers, there is no reliable air evacuation. Therefore, transport time can be very lengthy, depending on your location. Considering this, diving conservatively should go without saying: Do everything you can to avoid a dive accident!

Keep in mind that Hyperbaric Services Thailand charges more than US$800 per hour for treatment, so it is wise to purchase insurance before traveling. Despite rumors to the contrary, dive shops in Thailand do not offer recompression insurance.

Bangkok
Dept. of Underwater
   & Aviation Medicine
Phra Pinklao Naval Hospital
Taksin Road, Thonburi, Bangkok
☎ (2) 460 0000 through 0019, ext.
341, or (2) 460 1105; open 24 hours

Phuket
Hyperbaric Services Thailand
233 Rat-U-Thit 200 Pee Road,
Patong Beach, Phuket
☎ (76) 342 518 fax: (76) 342 519
After hours emergency number:
☎ (1) 693 1306
sssphk@loxinfo.co.th

Samui
Hyperbaric Services Thailand
34/8 Moo 4, Bo Phut, Ko Samui,
Surat Thani
☎ (77) 427 427 fax: (77) 427 377
After hours emergency number:
☎ (1) 606 3476
hstsamui@loxinfo.co.th

Pattaya Area
Khun Supachai (English speaking)
Apakorn Kiatiwong Naval Hospital
Sattahip, Chonburi Province
☎ (38) 437 171-2, or 862 1925;
26km east of Pattaya;
urgent care available 24 hours

DAN

Divers Alert Network (DAN) is an international membership association of individuals and organizations sharing a common interest in diving and safety. It includes DAN Southeast Asia and Pacific (DAN SEAP), an autonomous non-profit organization based in Australia. DAN operates a 24-hour diving emergency hotline. DAN SEAP members should call ☎ 61 8 8212 9242. DAN America members should call ☎ 919-684-8111 or 919-684-4DAN (-4326). The latter accepts collect calls in a dive emergency. Though DAN does not directly provide medical care, it does provide advice on early treatment, evacuation and hyperbaric treatment of diving-related injuries. Divers should contact DAN for assistance as soon as a diving emergency is suspected.

DAN membership is reasonably priced and includes DAN TravelAssist, a membership benefit that covers medical air evacuation from anywhere in the world for any illness or injury. For a small additional fee, divers can get secondary insurance coverage for decompression illness. For membership questions, contact DAN at ☎ 800-446-2671 in the U.S. or ☎ 919-684-2948 elsewhere. DAN can also be reached at www.diversalertnetwork.org.

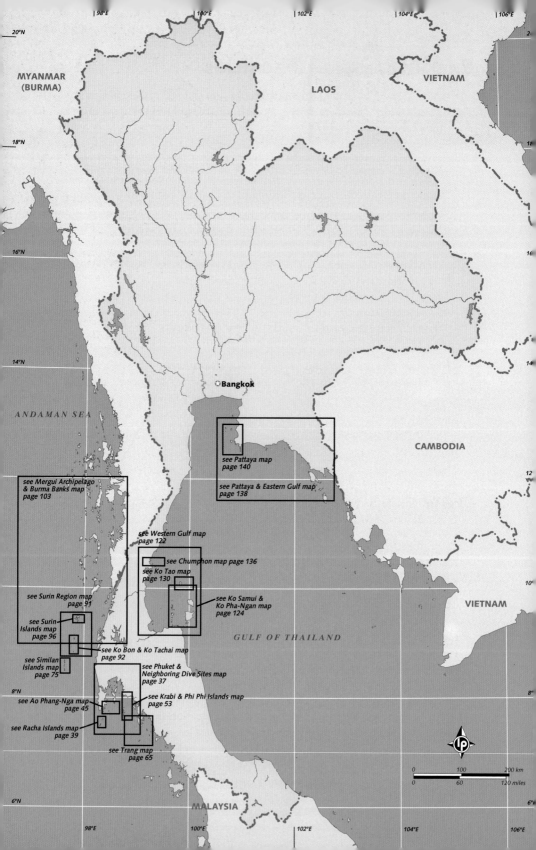

20°N

| 98°E

| 100°E

| 102°E

| 104°E

| 106°E

2

MYANMAR
(BURMA)

LAOS

VIETNAM

18°N

18

16°N

16

○ Bangkok

ANDAMAN SEA

14°N

14

CAMBODIA

12

see Pattaya map
page 140

see Mergui Archipelago
& Burma Banks map
page 103

see Pattaya & Eastern Gulf map
page 138

see Western Gulf map
page 122

see Chumphon map page 136

see Ko Tao map
page 130

VIETNAM

10

see Surin Region map
page 91

see Ko Samui &
Ko Pha-Ngan map
page 124

see Surin
Islands map
page 96

GULF OF THAILAND

see Ko Bon & Ko Tachai map
page 92

see Similan
Islands map
page 75

see Phuket &
Neighboring Dive Sites map
page 37

8°N

see Ao Phang-Nga map
page 45

see Krabi & Phi Phi Islands map
page 53

8°

see Racha Islands map
page 39

see Trang map
page 65

0   100   200 km
0   60   120 miles

6°N

MALAYSIA

6°

| 98°E

| 100°E

| 102°E

104°E

| 106°E

Diving in Thailand

MARK STRICKLAND

If Thailand's underwater attractions had to be summed up in one word, it would be "variety," both in terms of habitat and marine life. With more than 300 major reef groups covering an estimated area of 12,000 sq km (4,600 sq miles) in two oceans, it is easy to see why. Shallow coral gardens, steep island shorelines, pinnacles and submerged rocks are just a few of the environments divers will encounter. In addition, many areas offer specialized environments such as caverns and tunnels, including several true cave systems. And though Thailand is not especially well known for shipwrecks, a handful of diveable wrecks are easily reached by daytrip boats.

Thailand's waters are blessed with a great variety of fish and invertebrate life, ranging from tiny gobies, blennies and nudibranchs to giants like mantas and whale sharks. Many species are permanent residents at specific reefs, but most regions are also regularly visited by pelagics like rainbow runners, tuna and other oceanic nomads.

While Thailand's dive regions share some similarities, each has its own attractions and characteristics. Both the Andaman Sea (to the west) and the Gulf of Thailand (to the south and east) are popular with divers, but for very different reasons. For water clarity, scenic beauty, variety of dive sites and diversity of species, the Andaman Sea is the clear winner. However, the Gulf of Thailand has ample charms of its own, including a generally relaxed atmosphere, a wide selection of dive-training options and a profusion of marine life.

Live-Aboards

Thailand has many good diving and snorkeling sites within reach of daytrip boats, but most of the best reefs are at remote areas that require live-aboards to access. Completely self-contained, these vessels allow divers to maximize their underwater opportunities while minimizing travel time—usually by traveling long distances at night. Itineraries vary from one boat to the next, but range from two to ten days or more. Live-aboards that offer short trips generally specialize in one dive region, while extended itineraries often combine two or more regions. With a few exceptions, the vast majority of Thailand's live-aboard dive vessels are based in Phuket and service the Andaman Sea, accessing dive sites as far away as Myanmar's Mergui Archipelago and Burma Banks, and India's Andaman Islands. In the Gulf of Thailand, onshore accommodations combined with daytrips are the norm due to the relative closeness of dive sites, but a few live-aboard operations have started to provide two- to three-day trips from Pattaya to eastern gulf sites near Ko Chang and from Ko Samui to Ko Tao. From June through October, it may also be possible to join a live-aboard at Narathiwat to dive Ko Losin (near the Malaysian border) or from Nakorn Sri Thamarat for trips to Ko Kra.

Dive Boats

Just as dive programs and itineraries differ greatly, so do the choices of boats. There are wide variations in size, level of comfort and service, experience and knowledge of staff, atmosphere—and, of course, price. The good news is, no matter what your style, there's bound to be a boat for you.

Traditional wooden **longtail** boats are used throughout the country for virtually every kind of aquatic task, including diving and snorkeling trips. They get their name from the long propeller shaft that extends nearly 3m (10ft) behind the stern. While they work well enough for diving, longtails are notoriously tippy. It's best to stay seated while underway and keep a low center of gravity at all times. Back rolls are the preferred entry method, best done simultaneously by all divers on the count of three; this way the boat doesn't tip excessively, and you don't have to worry about landing on each other. When the dive is finished, hand your weight belt up to the crew, then scuba gear. Since few longtail boats are equipped with decent ladders, fins should be left on to help get you back aboard. To accomplish this, place both hands on the gunwale and kick gently until both legs are more or less horizontal on the surface. Then, in one big effort, kick down with both legs while pulling your body up with your arms. This nearly always does the trick, but if not, don't worry—the crew will gladly give you a hand. One final tip: If you disembark

MARK STRICKLAND

Sailing yachts are a popular and enjoyable option for dive trips.

at a beach, don't grab the propeller shaft or exhaust pipe for balance—it is usually quite hot by the end of a trip.

Speedboats powered by large outboard motors are relative newcomers to the Thai diving scene. Used primarily for daytrips, they are considerably faster than typical dive vessels, making them a good choice for more-distant sites, provided seas are relatively calm. In rough seas, however, these boats are forced to slow down, negating most advantages over more-traditional craft. Bear in mind that fuel consumption on these boats tends to be quite high, so expect correspondingly high trip prices.

Rigid inflatable boats or "RIBs" are often used for round-trips when a liveaboard is anchored away from a site, but a more common practice is for divers to enter from the mother ship and be picked up with the RIB. These days, they are also used for daytrips, particularly from Ko Tao and Ko Phi Phi. These boats can be tricky to get in and out of, so make sure you are briefed on appropriate and safe usage.

Converted fishing boats are the workhorses of many diving, snorkeling and sightseeing companies. They are generally of wooden construction and range from 9 to 30m (30 to 100ft) long. Features and amenities vary greatly from one boat to the next. When used for daytrips, such vessels are usually equipped with dive ladders, toilets, freshwater showers or rinse containers, a refreshment area and some kind of weather protection. Those serving as live-aboards generally have more extensive features such as a sundeck, galley and dining area and, of course, beds. Accommodations tend to be fairly spartan, with dormitory-style bunks or semi-private cabins. However, locally made boats are improving rapidly—both in safety and comfort features. Many boats in this class now offer private cabins with en suite bathrooms, and most have air-conditioning.

While seldom used for daytrip diving, **sailing yachts** are a popular and enjoyable option for live-aboard trips. Typically accommodating four to ten guests, these boats provide a chance to combine diving and snorkeling with a bit of sailing, fulfilling many people's dream of a well-rounded tropical getaway. Accommodations range from simple to opulent. Due to compressor size limitations, cruising speed and other factors, many sailing vessels do not offer as many dives per day as powerboats, yet they often compensate with more chances for island exploration and time under sail.

As Thailand's dive industry continues to grow, increasing competition and consumer demand have fueled a steady trend toward improved boats, with something to suit virtually every taste and budget. Most of this newest generation of "**purpose-designed dive boats**" are presently working as live-aboards, but it seems likely that daytrip operations will make similar upgrades in the near future. Even on the lower end of the price scale, most of these boats are equipped with lots of diver-oriented features like camera tables and rinse tanks, custom gear-storage areas, video and stereo systems and air-conditioned cabins. Among the more luxurious vessels, features often include freshwater makers, dedicated photo areas, video lounges, a library, film processing and video editing facilities, onboard photo/video pros, hot-water showers and private cabins (many with bathrooms en suite). Diving boats in Thailand are getting more sophisticated, and you should expect to see more and more of these boats coming into use very soon.

Thailand's Feature Creatures

Aside from a general abundance of marine life, Thailand's coral reefs also offer a chance to see some especially interesting and unusual creatures. Among invertebrates, some of the most fascinating are mantis shrimp, which posses highly specialized compound eyes capable of rotating 360°; the shrimp can strike prey with lightning speed. Another interesting crustacean is the tiny boxer crab, which carries a venomous sea anemone in each claw to fend off would-be attackers. Cephalopods like squid, octopuses and cuttlefish are all intelligent and fascinating animals, but the latter may win the prize for entertainment value. When courting, cuttlefish are quite unafraid of divers and often put on a mesmerizing display of color changes.

Naturally, there are fish that stand out from the others in terms of "personality" or unusual behavior. Perhaps the most familiar of these is the seahorse, though they are actually quite rare in most areas. Aside from their curious appearance, seahorses are unusual because of their monogamous relationship with their mates and the fact that only male seahorses give birth. A close relative, the beautiful harlequin ghost pipefish is so well camouflaged that it is often mistaken for a crinoid arm or gorgonian branch. There are also several endemic species, including the shy blue-spotted jawfish and the distinctive Andaman sweetlips.

MARK STRICKLAND
Mantis shrimp can rotate their eyes 360°.

Snorkeling

Thailand has some excellent snorkeling sites, and most beach resort areas have at least reasonable snorkeling nearby. While some of these sites are accessible from shore, many require boat access. Arranging this is normally quite easy: Just scout around until you find where the local longtail boats are anchored, start asking about snorkel trips, and within a few minutes someone is bound to walk up and offer to take you out.

Many of the best snorkeling spots (like the best dive sites) are beyond the range of daytrips. If you are interested in snorkeling one of these distant sites, it is often possible to join a live-aboard dive trip; passengers who are only snorkeling can sometimes get a reduced fare. Be sure to ask about the depth of the reefs. Though some of the shallow reefs are very healthy and attractive—especially in the Similan

Snorkelers explore Ao Maya (Maya Bay), Phi Phi Lae.

and Surin Islands, as well as at Ko Tao—at many top dive sites the best coral and marine life is moderately deep, often 12 to 24m (40 to 80ft). Unless you are an excellent free-diver, these places don't have much to offer the average snorkeler.

If you join a dive trip, decent quality rental snorkel gear is likely to be available. However, many of the sightseeing tours that offer snorkeling along with other activities provide poor quality gear—and poor quality service (e.g., no guides or knowledgeable staff). For such trips you are better off bringing your own gear. A few companies, especially in Phuket, now offer personalized, high-end snorkeling trips that may also include a beach barbecue, canoeing or other family-oriented activities.

Thailand's Top 10 Snorkeling Spots

9	Shark Point (Hin Mu Sang), Phuket
16	Hin Pae (Long Beach), Ko Phi Phi
17	Maya Bay, Ko Phi Phi
27	Eastern Shallows, Ko Similan #1
37	Beacon Beach, Ko Similan #8
48	Richelieu Rock, Surin region
49	Ko Torinla, Surin Marine National Park
51	Turtle Ledges, Surin region
64	Sail Rock (Hin Bai), Ko Samui
67	Red Rock (Shark Island), Ko Tao

Certification

Thailand is a great place to learn how to dive or continue your dive education. The water is warm, the marine life plentiful and the atmosphere relaxed and friendly. The popularity of diving here has encouraged dive services to improve their operations to remain competitive. What this means for students is extremely high standards of instruction, quality facilities and equipment and competitive pricing. Dive centers across the country offer a wide range of courses, from introductory dives to Divemaster programs. Most dive centers and liveaboards also offer Advanced Open Water certification and specialty courses. A number of technical diving programs are available, with courses regularly offered for Enriched Air Nitrox, Deep Air and even Rebreather Diving. Certification organizations include PADI, NAUI, BSAC, CMAS and others.

While course fees vary from one operator to the next, most entry-level courses cost from 6,000 to 11,000 baht (including rental equipment and possibly course materials) and typically take from two to four days to complete. Another option is to complete the classroom and pool sessions at home and perform the required Open Water dives in Thailand. This approach is known as a warm water (or student) referral and—provided all necessary documentation is in order—is fully sanctioned by most training agencies.

Dive Site Icons

The symbols at the beginning of each dive site description provide a quick summary of some of the important characteristics of each site:

 Good snorkeling or free-diving site.

 Remains or partial remains of a wreck can be seen at this site.

 Sheer wall or drop-off.

 Deep dive. Features of this dive are found in water deeper than 27m (90ft).

 Strong currents may be encountered at this site.

 Strong surge (the horizontal movement of water caused by waves) may be encountered at this site.

 Drift dive. Because of strong currents and/or difficulty in anchoring, a drift dive is recommended at this site.

 Shore dive. This site can be accessed from shore.

 Poor visibility. This site often has visibility of less than 8m (25ft).

 Caves or caverns are prominent features of this site. Only experienced cave divers should explore inner cave areas.

 Marine preserve. Special protective regulations apply in this area.

Pisces Rating System for Dives & Divers

The dive sites in this book are rated according to the following diver skill-level rating system. These are not absolute ratings but apply to divers at a particular time, diving at a particular place. For instance, someone unfamiliar with prevailing conditions might be considered a novice diver at one dive area, but an intermediate diver at another, more familiar location.

Novice: A novice diver should be accompanied by an instructor, divemaster or advanced diver on all dives. A novice diver generally fits the following profile:
◆ basic scuba certification from an internationally recognized certifying agency
◆ dives infrequently (less than one trip a year)
◆ logged fewer than 25 dives total
◆ little or no experience diving in similar waters and conditions
◆ dives no deeper than 18m (60ft)

Intermediate: An intermediate diver generally fits the following profile:
◆ may have participated in some form of continuing diver education
◆ logged between 25 and 100 dives
◆ dives no deeper than 40m (130ft)
◆ has been diving in similar waters and conditions within the last six months

Advanced: An advanced diver generally fits the following profile:
◆ advanced certification
◆ has been diving for more than two years and logged over 100 dives
◆ has been diving in similar waters and conditions within the last six months

Regardless of your skill level, you should be in good physical condition and know your limitations. If you are uncertain of your own level of expertise for a particular site, ask the advice of a local dive instructor. He or she is best qualified to assess your abilities based on the site's prevailing dive conditions. Ultimately, however, you must decide if you are capable of making a particular dive, a decision that should take into account your level of training, recent experience and physical condition, as well as the conditions at the site. Remember that conditions can change at any time, even during a dive.

Phuket & Neighboring Dive Sites

With its pleasant climate, expansive white-sand beaches and generally relaxed atmosphere, it is easy to see how Phuket (pronounced poo-KEht) has become one of Southeast Asia's premier resort areas. Often referred to as "The Pearl of the South," this tropical island rests on the eastern edge of the Andaman Sea, at the geographical heel of Thailand's boot-shaped peninsula. Phuket is connected to the rest of the kingdom by a bridge at its northernmost point, where the narrow Chong Pak Phra channel flows between the two landmasses. Covering 810 sq km (313 sq miles), it is the country's largest island—about the size of Singapore.

In spite of rapid development in recent years, Phuket remains rich in natural beauty. Much of the landscape consists of steep hills, some of which are still clad in verdant jungle. A sizable tract of this pristine forest is now protected as a national park. Common rural scenes include shady green rubber-tree forests, fertile rice paddies and herds of docile water buffalo accompanied by slender white egrets. Spectacular limestone islands surrounded by emerald waters dot the horizon off Phuket's east shore. On the west coast, clear blue seas lap against white-sand beaches, separated by rocky coves and headlands.

Longtail boat at Maya Bay.

Phuket is well known for its diverse marine life and healthy coral reefs, providing outstanding diving and snorkeling opportunities. The closest are Phuket's **west coast** sites. While visibility is seldom very good, the west coast offers reasonably healthy coral reefs within a few minutes' travel time from shore. Farther afield, south of Phuket, the **Racha Islands** provide fair to excellent diving and snorkeling with good visibility and sites that suit divers of all experience levels and interests. East of Phuket, a handful of sites in **Ao Phang-Nga** (Phang-Nga Bay) offer a variety of underwater terrain, along with perhaps the richest and most diverse marine life in the region. This is also the home of one of Phuket's most recent dive acquisitions, the *King Cruiser* wreck. **Krabi** and the **Phi Phi Islands** are also within reach of Phuket dive boats, but the daytrip from Phuket is a long one, usually averaging 2 to 3 hours one way.

With few exceptions, daytrips leave from Ao Chalong, on the southeast side of Phuket. Most trips depart between 8 and 9am, offer two dives and lunch, and return mid to late afternoon.

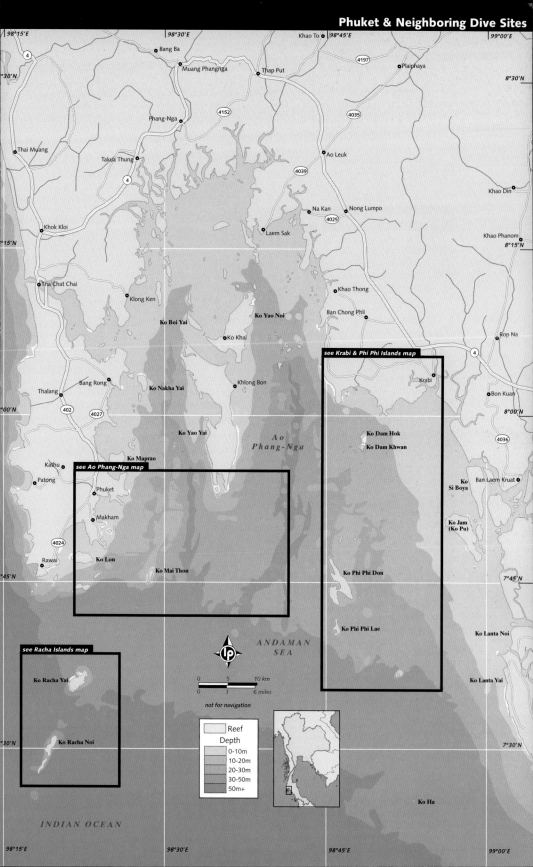

98°15'E
98°30'E
98°45'E
99°00'E

8°30'N

Khao To

Bang Ba
4197
Plaiphaya
Muang Phangnga
Thap Put
4
Phang-Nga
4152
4035
Thai Muang
Ao Leuk
Takua Thung
4
4039

8°15'N

Khao Din

Khao Phanom

Khok Kloi
Na Kan
Nong Lumpo
4025
Laem Sak

Tha Chat Chai
Khao Thong
Klong Ken
Ban Chong Phli

Ko Boi Yai
Ko Yao Noi
Rop Na
Ko Khai

see Krabi & Phi Phi Islands map

Bang Rong
4
Thalang
Ko Nakha Yai
Khlong Bon
Krabi
402
4027
Bon Kuan

8°00'N

Ko Yao Yai
Ao
Phang-Nga
Ko Dam Hok
4036
Ko Dam Khwan

Ko Maprao
see Ao Phang-Nga map
Kathu
Ko
Ban Laem Kruat
Phuket
Si Boya
Patong
Makham
Ko Jam
(Ko Pu)
4024
Rawai
Ko Lon
Ko Mai Thon
Ko Phi Phi Don

7°45'N

see Racha Islands map
Ko Phi Phi Lae
Ko Lanta Noi

ANDAMAN
SEA
Ko Racha Yai

Ko Lanta Yai

7°30'N

Ko Racha Noi

0   5   10 km
0   3   6 miles

not for navigation

Reef
Depth
0-10m
10-20m
20-30m
30-50m
50m+

Ko Ha

INDIAN OCEAN

98°15'E
98°30'E
98°45'E
99°00'E

Several companies now offer half-day trips via speedboat to the normal daytrip sites (except Ko Phi Phi), with departure times in either the morning or afternoon. Prices for daytrips generally include tanks, weights, lunch and snacks, and transport to and from local (Phuket) accommodations.

Ko Phi Phi's dive shops all offer daytrips to the popular spots around the Phi Phi Islands and to Ao Phang-Nga's Shark Point (Hin Muang), Anemone Reef and

Phuket's West Coast

Although Phuket's east coast is too silty for diving or snorkeling, most of the west-facing shores support some healthy and enjoyable coral growth. Though not great reefs, they offer convenient access, easy conditions and a surprisingly good variety of marine life. Ideally suited for dive training, these places are also great for casual excursions via longtail boat, combining snorkeling, diving and lunch on an isolated beach. Though relatively few operators offer dedicated dive trips here, things are much easier to organize for snorkeling excursions—simply walk to where the longtail boats are anchored and ask around. Chances are you won't have to look far before someone expresses interest in shuttling you to a snorkeling spot.

Most of the reefs are within 5 to 20 minutes' travel time from popular west coast beaches. Among the better known sites are **Ko Pu** (a small island off Kata Beach), **Karon Pinnacle** (Karon Beach), **Paradise Reef** (Patong Beach), **Nakalay** (Kalim), **Amanpuri Reef** (between Surin and Bang Tao beaches) and **Ko Waeo** (Bang Tao Beach). Typical marine life includes various hard corals, anemones, nudibranchs, sea stars and many other invertebrates. Most sites also have a variety of reef fish such as lionfish, anemonefish, damselfish, wrasse, groupers, snappers, sweetlips, lizardfish, triggerfish and many others. Occasionally, divers see unusual species like ribbon eels or razorfish; even whale sharks have been known to make an appearance.

An interesting wreck dive known as **Tin Lizzy** is just a few minutes' boat ride from Bang Tao Beach. This working tin dredge sank in the early 1990s at the onset of the southwest monsoon. The hull sits upright in about 15m (50ft) of water, lying north to south. Though the wreck can't be penetrated, there are many intact elements worth seeing: On deck, the dredge buckets and conveyer belt are clearly recogniz-

able. Fish life includes schools of five-lined snappers, young yellowtail barracuda, honeycomb morays, porcupine pufferfish, flatheads, lionfish and lots of scorpionfish. This is also among the few places where you can see true stonefish. Invertebrates include cuttlefish, octopuses and an abundance of murices and other shellfish. As on most wrecks, there are plenty of sharp surfaces and lots of barnacles, so move slowly and carefully when diving here.

MARK STRICKLAND

the *King Cruiser*. Krabi's dive centers offer similar services, but the rides to the better spots are longer.

In addition to offering some very good local diving, this scenic island serves as a departure point for the majority of Thailand's live-aboard fleet. As the gateway to the Andaman Sea, Phuket provides access to most of the best diving in Thailand, as well as Myanmar's Mergui Archipelago and Burma Banks, and India's Andaman Islands.

Racha Islands

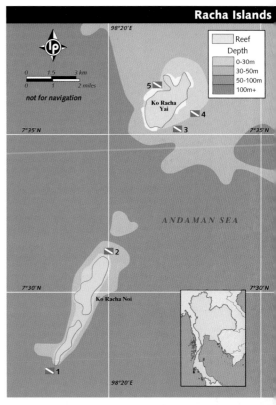

The Racha area (sometimes spelled *Raya*) consists of two main islands, Ko Racha Yai and Ko Racha Noi. Both are popular diving destinations, but for very different reasons.

Racha Yai (*yai* means "big" in Thai) is known for its clear water, healthy marine life and generally easy, year-round diving. Because of these typically gentle conditions, this island is a prime choice for dive training and snorkeling and offers a suitable environment for divers of all experience levels. Most of the better sites are along the east coast, which is protected from the southwest monsoon. Dive sites primarily consist of sloping hard-coral reefs surrounded by white-sand bottoms.

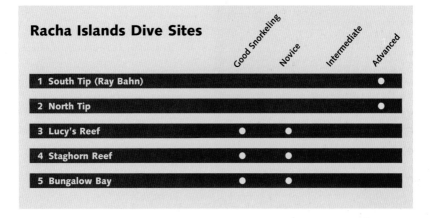

Racha Islands Dive Sites	Good Snorkeling	Novice	Intermediate	Advanced
1 South Tip (Ray Bahn)				●
2 North Tip				●
3 Lucy's Reef	●	●		
4 Staghorn Reef	●	●		
5 Bungalow Bay	●	●		

Marine life includes a variety of reef fish and invertebrates. It is also quite scenic above water, with several superb white-sand beaches bordered by groves of coconut trees. Bungalows are available for those who wish to stay on the island.

Racha Noi ("small" Racha) usually enjoys good visibility like its bigger neighbor to the north, but offers more rugged and dramatic underwater scenery as well as a better chance for big-animal encounters. Although it is normally referred to as a single destination, Racha Noi actually consists of two islands, separated by a narrow pass.

Though diving at Racha Noi is often easy and relaxed, some days the current can prove rather challenging, even for experienced divers. To take advantage of the current, most dives start on the up-current end of the reef, allowing you to drift along and get picked up at the down-current end. It is essential to have some kind of surface marker, as currents can be strong and changeable at times. Occasionally, vertical down-currents exist, requiring extra effort to stay within a planned maximum depth. Because of these variable and sometimes difficult conditions, inexperienced divers should think twice before joining a trip to this area.

1 South Tip (Ray Bahn)

Although Racha Noi's entire perimeter offers reasonably good diving, the best and most popular sites are at the extreme north and south ends of the island.

The South Tip is an exciting, scenic dive that is well worth the extra half hour to hour required to reach it. Reef topography consists of rocky slopes, coral gardens, and rock pinnacles that reach within 12m of the surface. Soft corals are

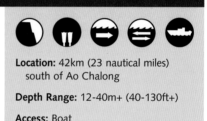

Location: 42km (23 nautical miles) south of Ao Chalong

Depth Range: 12-40m+ (40-130ft+)

Access: Boat

Expertise Rating: Advanced

much more prolific here than at any other Racha Islands site, and while generally small, their pastel pink, purple and lavender hues add a great deal of color to the scenery. Perhaps it is these soft corals, along with the rocky terrain, that leads many divers to compare this site with Similan Islands sites.

Fish life is impressive here, with plenty of resident reef dwellers like squirrelfish, snappers, lionfish and moray eels. Schooling fish such as chevron barracuda, blue-fin jacks and rainbow runners make regular appearances. Be sure to

MARK STRICKLAND
Giant squirrelfish are colorful but secretive.

have a look around the deeper areas, as marbled stingrays, leopard sharks and whitetip reef sharks can often be seen resting on the bottom. South Tip offers the best chance of any Phuket-area reef to see manta rays, though they are not common. Whale sharks also make occasional appearances here.

2 North Tip

At North Tip, the main dive site consists of a submerged, rocky ridge that extends well away from the island to the north. Underwater terrain is similar to South Tip but shallower, with rocky slopes, coral gardens and huge rock pinnacles that start at the surface and plunge almost vertically to beyond recreational diving depths, allowing perfect multilevel profiles. Marine life includes hard and soft corals, pillow and feather stars, various crabs and shrimp and a variety of reef fish.

It is worth keeping an eye trained toward the open water here, as jacks and barracuda are frequently cruising by just

Location: 34km (18 nautical miles) south of Ao Chalong

Depth Range: 5-36m+ (16-118ft+)

Access: Boat

Expertise Rating: Advanced

beyond the reef, and mantas are always a possibility. Whitetip reef sharks and marbled stingrays are sometimes seen in deeper areas. As with South Tip, currents can be very strong here, occasionally including vertical up- or down-currents.

MARK STRICKLAND

Marbled stingrays are sometimes seen in deeper areas.

3 Lucy's Reef

Lucy's Reef is a popular east side site along the fringing reef parallel to Racha Yai. Possibly the best of Yai's dive sites, this sloping reef is composed of numerous hard-coral species and a few soft corals.

Marine life is somewhat more diverse here than at nearby sites, with a good representation of invertebrates like nudibranchs, anemones, sea stars and mantis shrimp. Reef fish—including titan and orange-lined triggerfish, emperor angelfish, trumpetfish and several species of lionfish—are also abundant. Occasionally, unusual species like frogfish and cockatoo waspfish are encountered here, and even leopard sharks are sporadically seen. While this site is not known for its pelagics, manta rays and whale sharks are seen on rare occasions.

Although currents are usually slight in this area, there is often sufficient flow to provide a gentle boost as you fin along the reef. Accordingly, drift diving is a popular technique, and most dives are conducted as one-way excursions, typically from north to south.

Location: 25km (13 nautical miles) south of Ao Chalong

Depth Range: 5-27m (16-89ft)

Access: Boat

Expertise Rating: Novice

Snorkeling is good all along Racha Yai's east coast, especially between Lucy's Reef and Staghorn Reef, where there tends to be less current than in other areas. Healthy coral growth reaches within a few meters of the surface.

Both Lucy's Reef and Staghorn Reef are normally accessible throughout the year, but are especially well located for the southwest monsoon, when they are completely protected from prevailing wind and seas. During the northeast monsoon, conditions can get choppy along the east coast, making west-facing sites like Bungalow Bay a better choice.

4 Staghorn Reef

One of several good sites on Racha Yai's east side, Staghorn is north of Lucy's Reef on the fringing, hard coral reef that runs parallel to the shore. In keeping with its name, this site consists mostly of staghorn and fire corals surrounded by white sand and occasional rock formations.

You'll find a range of marine life, including invertebrates such as crinoids, sea cucumbers and octopuses. Fish are plentiful, with schooling species like yellowtail barracuda, fusiliers and twin-spot snappers hovering over the coral. Reef

Location: 25km (13 nautical miles) south of Ao Chalong

Depth Range: 5-27m (16-89ft)

Access: Boat

Expertise Rating: Novice

dwellers are also in good supply, including giant morays, goatfish and various species of butterflyfish and wrasse. While currents here are not as dependable as at Lucy's Reef, conditions often allow for gentle, one-way drift dives.

At Staghorn's south end (toward Lucy's Reef), you'll find especially good snorkeling conditions. The current is normally less strong here than at other areas along Racha Yai's east coast, and the coral reaches to within a few meters of the surface.

5 Bungalow Bay

Bungalow Bay is on Racha Yai's west side and is probably the island's most frequently dived site.

Above the surface, the scenery matches most people's expectations of what tropical paradise ought to look like: sparkling blue water, white-sand beaches and coconut trees galore. Below the surface, the reef is not as spectacular, yet is very popular because of the dependably easy conditions, at least during the northeast monsoon season. Not surprisingly, this is a favorite dive-training area and is especially appropriate for novice divers and snorkelers.

Location: 25km (13 nautical miles) south of Ao Chalong

Depth Range: 5-30m (16-98ft)

Access: Boat

Expertise Rating: Novice

Most diving takes place along the rocky shoreline on the north side of the bay, which slopes down to a sand bottom at 10 to 30m, depending on the area. Underwater terrain consists mostly of

MARK STRICKLAND

This fried egg nudibranch is laying a spiral egg case.

granite rocks with intermittent growths of staghorn, dome and leather coral.

Although not especially well known for "critters," Bungalow Bay is an excellent place for nudibranchs, including some species seldom seen at other sites. Fish life includes black-spotted pufferfish, lionfish, parrotfish and moray eels, as well as passing schools of blue-fin jacks and fusiliers. On rare occasions, unusual species like robust ghost pipefish are encountered here, typically hovering over the seafloor; there have also been reports of razorfish hovering vertically among branching corals, and bizarre-looking seamoths (Pegasus fish), which blend in perfectly with the sandy bottom. A more dependable highlight is the abundance of blue-spotted stingrays. Often as you swim along the reef's deeper edges, one ray after another will explode out of the sand, then flee the scene at warp speed.

Ao Phang-Nga

Ao Phang-Nga (Phang-Nga Bay) is bounded by Krabi Province to the east, Phang-Nga Province to the northwest and Phuket to the west. Because only its south side faces the open sea, this area is better protected from rough seas than most, especially during the northeast monsoon. Another advantage offered by Ao Phang-Nga is its proximity to the Phuket resort area. As with Racha and the West Coast, dive sites are close enough to be accessed as daytrips, making it

The stunning vertical rock formations continue beneath Ao Phang-Nga's surface.

possible to enjoy good diving without giving up the comforts of life on land. While these factors have done much to make this area popular, the main reason to dive here is the impressive abundance and diversity of marine life—by far the best in the Phuket region. Although visibility is seldom great, there are plenty of attractions, including fascinating and varied underwater terrain, prolific fish life and a wealth of invertebrates.

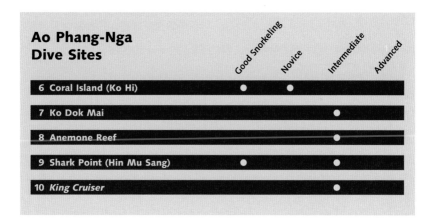

Ao Phang-Nga Dive Sites	Good Snorkeling	Novice	Intermediate	Advanced
6 Coral Island (Ko Hi)	●	●		
7 Ko Dok Mai			●	
8 Anemone Reef			●	
9 Shark Point (Hin Mu Sang)	●		●	
10 King Cruiser			●	

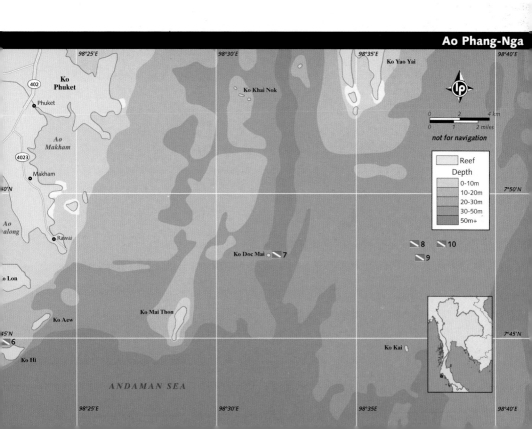

Ao Phang-Nga

6 Coral Island (Ko Hi)

Just a 15- to 30-minute boat ride from Ao Chalong (southern Phuket), Coral Island is one of the region's most accessible dive sites and is among its most heavily promoted and frequently visited. Though the area may disappoint seasoned divers, the generally calm seas make Coral Island a good choice for novices. Because of its sheltered location, this is also among the few Phuket daytrip sites that can be dived year-round, almost regardless of weather conditions.

Diving at Coral Island takes place off the two white-sand beaches on the north side and at the rocky points at the east and west tips of the island. Although visibility is normally poor to fair (only 2 to 10m), hard-coral growth is quite good in some areas, and you'll find a surprising variety of reef fish as well. There are also

Location: 7.5km (4 nautical miles) south-southeast of Ao Chalong

Depth Range: 0-21m (0-69ft)

Access: Shore or boat

Expertise Rating: Novice

good snorkeling possibilities here, especially on the island's south side.

A word of warning: Boating traffic can be heavy, especially near the north-side beaches. Longtail boats and jet skis are a serious safety hazard. When possible, stay submerged (at a minimum depth of 5m) until you return to the mooring line, or if diving from the beach, until you are back in very shallow water.

7 Ko Doc Mai

Even from miles away, Ko Doc Mai, which means "Island of Flowers" in Thai, is an imposing sight, as the steep cliffs of this small island tower far above the sea. Underwater, the scenery can be equally impressive, with dramatic topography and abundant marine life.

Upon entering the water on the north, east or south sides of the island, you will find coral-encrusted walls that drop almost vertically to a sandy bottom at 27 to 30m. On the west side, the underwater terrain slopes more gently, giving this part of the site a completely different feel. A perfect multilevel dive, this site offers great scenery at every depth from the bottom right up to the surface. While visibility averages only 5 to 15m, it may occasionally reach 24m

Location: About 21km (11 nautical miles) east of Ao Chalong

Depth Range: 0-33m (0-108ft)

Access: Boat

Expertise Rating: Intermediate

or better. At those times, this is indeed a spectacular dive.

Like Shark Point and Anemone Reef, Ko Doc Mai is an officially designated fisheries reserve. All marine life within these areas is protected, though in practice, regulations are seldom enforced.

Marine life is varied and healthy, including a wide range of invertebrates like golden wentletrap snails, zig-zag oysters, barrel sponges, black corals, nudibranchs, sea whips, gorgonians and various hard corals.

When the current is running, the south and east sides can be especially scenic, as the wall seems to blossom with orange cup corals that open up to feed. The north side is also very attractive at such times, due to the abundant soft corals.

Fish life is extensive, including blue-lined groupers, lunar wrasse, blue-ringed angelfish, several species of morays and a host of other colorful species.

Watch where you place your hands here, as scorpionfish and lionfish are very common, and both are quite talented at blending in with

MARK STRICKLAND

Diver looks at colorful gorgonians along Ko Doc Mai's steep wall.

the scenery. Also among the local camouflage experts are two unusual and uncommon species—tigertail seahorses and harlequin ghost pipefish, both of which tend to hang out amid black corals and gorgonians.

From time to time, you'll also see leopard sharks sleeping on the sandy bottom or cruising gracefully along the reef. Banded sea snakes are frequently encountered as they browse amid the

corals or sun themselves on the rocks at water's edge.

Two large caverns and several smaller crevices punctuate the wall on the island's east side. It is worth having a look at the sponge- and shellfish-covered walls and ceiling of the largest cave, which extends at least 15m into the island. It is best to stay close to the exit, as visibility can drop to zero if a diver kicks up the silty bottom.

8 Anemone Reef

Anemone Reef's rocky pinnacle is a small-scale, completely submerged version of its neighbor, Shark Point, which lies less than a kilometer to the south. True to its name, shallow portions of this site are absolutely covered with a living carpet of sea anemones. Some are lime-green or brown, others vivid pink; together they create an almost surrealistic impression as they wave back and forth in the surge. Of course, nature would never allow so many potential homes to sit vacant—porcelain crabs, shrimp and five varieties of anemonefish inhabit the anemones.

Anemones are certainly not all that this prolific reef has to offer. Soft corals, gorgonians, bivalves, crabs, shrimp and other invertebrates populate the rocky slopes. Fish life includes just about everything that swims; butterflyfish, angelfish, wrasse and sweetlips browse amid the corals, while groupers, snappers and

Location: 30km (16 nautical miles) east of Ao Chalong; 19km (10 nautical miles) west of Ko Phi Phi Don

Depth Range: 4-24m (13-79ft)

Access: Boat

Expertise Rating: Intermediate

meter-long queenfish terrorize clouds of glassfish in the shallows. Leopard sharks, seen here quite regularly, usually rest on the sandy bottom near the reef's edge.

Another of Anemone Reef's attractions is a remarkable abundance of lionfish—sometimes more than a dozen within a one-square-meter area! When the current is running, these teams of attractive predators spread their delicate but venomous fins out like fans to herd and devour small baitfish.

MARK STRICKLAND

Anemone Reef is covered with a living carpet of sea anemones.

Rising from depths of around 22 to 24m, Anemone Reef tops out at about 4m, making for good multilevel profiles. Visibility ranges from 8 to 21m, averaging about 10m. Although currents can be quite strong at times, the large rock structure provides shelter; there is always a protected side where currents are slight.

Anemone Reef and neighboring Shark Point were officially designated as the Hin Mu Sang Fisheries Reserve in 1992. Accordingly, these areas are protected by law. It is illegal to anchor, fish or collect any marine life here. Moorings have helped reduce destructive anchoring practices in this area—it is rare to see boats anchored on the reef. Unfortunately, enforcement of other regulations is still sorely lacking; hopefully the situation will improve in the future.

9 Shark Point (Hin Mu Sang)

Home to an incredible profusion of marine life, Shark Point easily ranks among the richest marine habitats in the Phuket region. Nearly every square inch of this site is inhabited, providing a density and diversity of reef creatures that is seldom seen.

Location: 30km (16 nautical miles) east of Ao Chalong; 19km (10 nautical miles) west of Ko Phi Phi Don

Depth Range: 0-24m (0-79ft)

Access: Boat

Expertise Rating: Intermediate

Although it actually consists of three narrowly separated reefs, Shark Point is usually referred to as a single dive site. At the northernmost of these reefs, a small portion of rock sticks out a few meters above the surface, providing a good reference point. All three reefs are composed of rocky, coral-covered outcroppings protruding from a sand and shell bottom.

In deeper areas, mushroom corals and long-spine sea urchins lie scattered about, accompanied by stands of whip coral and some fairly large gorgonians. Brilliant soft corals adorn almost every rock, especially around the shallower portions of the middle reef. Interspersed with the soft corals are sponges, feather stars and various bivalves, all relentlessly competing for space.

In the shallower depths, hard corals cover many areas, along with a large number of sea anemones. Shimmering silver clouds of glassfish cluster around rocks and coral to avoid the squadrons of ravenous jacks, mackerel and snappers that constantly patrol the area. Meanwhile, patient predators like honeycomb groupers and scorpionfish lie in ambush, waiting for their meals to come to them. At virtually every depth, moray eels peek from crevices, while a wide selection of colorful reef fish meander amid the corals. Cephalopods are relatively common here as well, and cuttlefish, octopuses and squid are frequently seen.

Among Shark Point's biggest attractions are the shy, amiable leopard sharks that the site was named for, often seen resting along the sandy edges of the reef. Also known as zebra sharks, these animals are far from the stereotypical image that most people have of sharks, as they pose absolutely no threat to humans. With their small mouth and tiny teeth, leopard sharks would have trouble biting you even if they wanted to. They prefer to prowl the reef in search of their favorite prey—crustaceans and mollusks—rather than chase divers.

Because divers can often approach them quite closely, leopard sharks are tremendously popular. Regrettably, the animals' trusting attitude often causes them to suffer at the hands of divers. As the sharks normally rest on the bottom during daylight hours, many divers can't resist tugging on their tails, grabbing fins or generally harassing them. While this may seem like harmless fun to the divers involved, it is bound to be a frightening and aggravating experience for the sharks. If divers persist with such behavior, the sharks will likely leave the area for good. It may be tempting to touch these animals as they lie peacefully on the bottom, but discerning divers know better—please look, but do not touch!

Even if you don't see a leopard shark, Shark Point still ranks as an outstanding dive. Depths are moderate, with excellent marine life ranging from a maximum of 24m all the way to the surface. While currents can be fairly strong, they need not pose a problem. The large rock structures provide plenty of protection on their down-current sides; you should have no problem getting out of the flow.

Also, currents tend to run more or less lengthwise (north-south) along the three rocky outcroppings, and a drift dive will take advantage of this free ride. Be sure the boat crew understands that you need to be retrieved down-current. Although visibility here is not often great (averaging 8 to 12m), it can occasionally reach up to 24m. Regardless, the profusion of marine life at Shark Point makes this a don't-miss site.

Remember that Shark Point is part of the Hin Mu Sang Fisheries Reserve. It is illegal to anchor, fish or collect marine life here.

Shark Point was named for the leopard sharks often seen resting quietly on the sandy bottom.

10　*King Cruiser*

Despite abundant diving opportunities, the Phuket dive scene had, until recently, been lacking in one respect: There were no real wreck dives. An unexpected turn of events changed that situation in one fell swoop. On May 4, 1997, at about 10:15am, the *King Cruiser*—an 85m, steel-hulled, catamaran-style passenger ferry—struck the well-charted shoal Anemone Reef while running its regular route from Phuket to Ko Phi Phi.

Exactly why such an easily avoidable navigational error was made is still unknown, especially considering the flat, calm seas and perfect weather that day. In any case, the results were dramatic and immediate. The impact ripped a sizable hole in the bottom of the port hull and the vessel started taking on large volumes of water. Luckily, many local boats quickly arrived on the scene and offered assistance. Thanks to these boat opera-

Location: 32km (17 nautical miles) east of Ao Chalong; 17km (9 nautical miles) west of Ko Phi Phi Don

Depth Range: 12-33m (40-108ft)

Access: Boat

Expertise Rating: Intermediate

tors, along with the Thai Marine Police, all 539 passengers and 22 crew were successfully rescued; there was no loss of life. After drifting a little more than a kilometer from Anemone Reef, the ship finally slipped below the surface, where she settled sitting upright on the 32m deep bottom.

What was a disastrous event from a navigational standpoint turned out to be a blessing for the dive community. Within a week of sinking, the wreck was

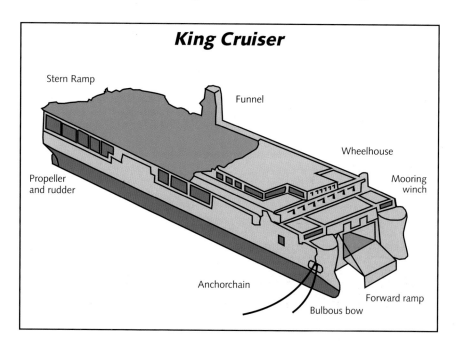

King Cruiser

Stern Ramp

Funnel

Wheelhouse

Propeller and rudder

Mooring winch

Anchorchain

Forward ramp

Bulbous bow

already attracting marine life, as schools of jacks and queenfish gathered to pursue the clouds of baitfish seeking shelter around the wreck. Reef species like cardinalfish, snappers, lionfish and scorpionfish moved in. Even frogfish have been seen here. Dense schools of juvenile barracuda have also taken up residence, especially in the wheelhouse. Though coral growth may take a number of years to become established, most of the hull is already covered with acorn barnacles—a good reason to wear gloves and move slowly at this site.

Unlike many wrecks, *King Cruiser* makes a good multilevel dive, as portions come within 12m of the surface. Most of the hull is reasonably safe to swim around, but you should resist the urge to explore inside, as sections collapse regularly, making penetration a very risky prospect.

Krabi & Phi Phi Islands

Over the years, Krabi and the province's most famous island group, Ko Phi Phi (pronounced pee-pee), have grown into one of Thailand's busiest tourist areas. Ko Phi Phi is about 45km (28 miles) east of Phuket, and Krabi is on the mainland about 30km (20 miles) north-northeast of Ko Phi Phi. You can reach Ko Phi Phi by ferry from Phuket, Krabi or Ko Lanta (an island to the southeast). Krabi can be reached by road or by ferry. Both are delightful places to spend a few days relaxing on exquisite beaches, exploring numerous coves and bays, climbing steep peaks and enjoying some colorful and alluring scuba diving.

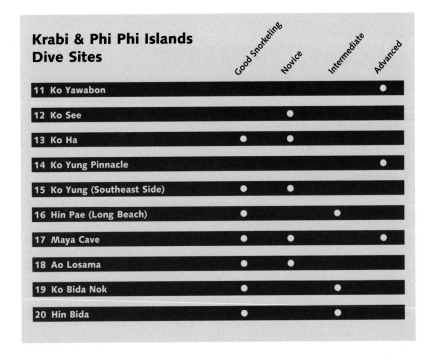

Krabi & Phi Phi Islands Dive Sites	Good Snorkeling	Novice	Intermediate	Advanced
11 Ko Yawabon				●
12 Ko See		●		
13 Ko Ha	●	●		
14 Ko Yung Pinnacle				●
15 Ko Yung (Southeast Side)	●	●		
16 Hin Pae (Long Beach)	●		●	
17 Maya Cave	●	●		●
18 Ao Losama	●	●		
19 Ko Bida Nok	●		●	
20 Hin Bida	●		●	

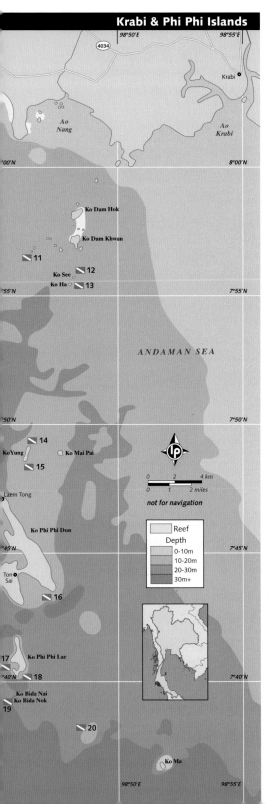

Krabi & Phi Phi Islands

Krabi has a few interesting dive sites, but most dive operators go to the Phi Phi Islands or (on a limited basis) to Trang dive sites farther south. The Phi Phi island group is composed of Ko Phi Phi Don (Hilly Island), Ko Phi Phi Lae (Phi Phi of the Sea), Ko Yung (Mosquito Island) and Ko Mai Pai (Bamboo Island). Ko Phi Phi Don, the largest of the group, is the only option for overnight accommodations and can be reached by ferry from Krabi and Phuket. All the islands are dived by daytrip operators out of Phuket, Krabi and Ko Phi Phi Don. Few live-aboards visit this area (though live-aboards to Hin Daeng usually stop at Ko Phi Phi), but overnight trips from Phuket to Ko Phi Phi can be arranged.

Topside, amazing limestone cliffs rise dramatically into the sky. The drama continues underwater, where divers can explore the fascinating topography: Over time the elements have eroded the soft rock to form caves, caverns, overhangs and swim-throughs. Vertical walls drop from the surface to beyond 25m. A profusion of soft corals, large orange sea fans, black coral and sea whips grows on these walls. Several types of unusual corals grow in the surrounding waters.

In many places, the Phi Phi Islands are fringed with hard-coral gardens. In most areas, coral growth and fish life (including five species of anemonefish) are profuse. Although visibility is seldom spectacular, the amount of marine life within the calm waters surrounding Ko Phi Phi should keep all but the most seasoned diver happy for a number of days. The enjoyable diving—along with the friendly way of life, beautiful beaches and fun island cruises in funky longtail boats—will continue to make this area one of Thailand's most popular destinations.

11 Ko Yawabon

This island is one of many where interesting tunnels and caves are found, but it is distinctive in that you can swim all the way through the island from one side to the other. Most dives start on the western side of Ko Yawabon, where you'll find protection from prevailing winds. You'll find the entrance to the primary tunnel at 6m. There is not much life in the tunnel due to lack of light, but it is a nice swim-through. As in all overhead environments, please use caution during a dive such as this. Be sure to exercise careful buoyancy control to avoid stirring up the silt and degrading visibility.

Besides the swim-through, the interesting bottom topography and variety of fish will please divers. Anemones and their clownfish companions, lion-

Location: 5km (2.7 nautical miles) south of Ao Nang

Depth Range: 3-20m (10-66ft)

Access: Boat

Expertise Rating: Advanced

fish, parrotfish and, very often, leopard sharks are seen here. Never approach leopard sharks from above, as this will frighten them and they are likely to swim away. Instead, approach leopard sharks at eye level and slowly move toward them. Often you can get within centimeters of a shark without startling it. Currents can be tricky, so be sure to listen to the divemaster's briefing.

Overhead Environments

The fascinating formations and marine life of Thailand's caves and caverns are usually a diver's dream, but can quickly turn into a nightmare if safety concerns are ignored. Strong surge, loss of light, disorientation and complicated interconnecting tunnel systems can be serious hazards for divers, but you can take precautions to reduce the risks of diving in overhead environments.

- A diver should only consider cave or cavern penetration after obtaining appropriate certification, or when accompanied by an experienced guide who is familiar with the cavern. Never dive in an overhead environment alone.

- Consult with your dive guide on any special safety equipment that may be needed and, of course, whether conditions are safe to dive.

- When in an overhead environment, move slowly and stay off the bottom to avoid kicking up silt and degrading the visibility. If you can't due to buoyancy control difficulties, do not enter an overhead environment.

- Unless cave certified, do not penetrate beyond the reach of natural light and always keep the entrance within view.

- Start to exit with at least two-thirds of your air supply remaining, and have at least one-third left when you finally do exit.

12 Ko See

Accessed from Ao Nang in Krabi (rather than from Ko Phi Phi), this is a popular site for divers of all expertise levels. One of many dramatic limestone rock islands rising out of Phang-Nga Bay, Ko See (meaning "Island Four") lies just north of Ko Ha ("Island Five"). Ko See, the larger of these two islands, features rocks and coral heads surrounded by sand patches between 6 and 12m, making it an ideal Open Water training site.

The currents can be strong here, so consult a tide table before diving. The best marine life is found at relatively shallow depths (12 to 15m), which allows enough bottom time to circumnavigate the island on one dive.

On the northwest side of the island, you'll find a wall with soft corals and sea whips clinging to it. Bubble coral,

Location: 9km (4.9 nautical miles) south of Ao Nang

Depth Range: 0-18m (0-59ft)

Access: Boat

Expertise Rating: Novice

which many people mistake for a type of anemone, is quite common at this site.

Leopard sharks are seen here most of the time, and a resident group of blacktip reef sharks hangs out in the area. Since blacktip reef sharks are normally shy around divers, you'll be more likely to get a closer look if you are snorkeling.

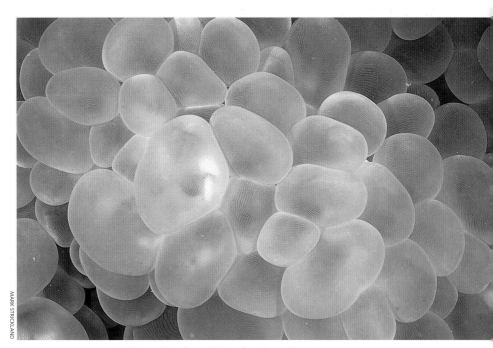

MARK STRICKLAND

Bubble coral is often mistaken for a type of anemone.

13 Ko Ha

This small, rocky island is similar to its northern neighbor, Ko See. Though Ko Ha is not as good for snorkeling (the best marine life is found below 5m), the dive is still a fairly shallow one. You are likely to have enough bottom time to completely circle the island in one dive.

Here, as at Ko See, leopard sharks rest in and swim near the sandy areas, and giant morays poke their heads from their protective holes in the reef. Bubble corals and sea anemones create a patchwork tapestry over the boulders and hard corals. This dive site also has more than its fair share of blue-spotted stingrays, mainly concentrated on the southern side of the island.

Banded sea snakes and "banded" snake eels are also quite common. Though these animals look very similar,

Location: 9.5km (5 nautical miles) south of Ao Nang

Depth Range: 5-20m (16-66ft)

Access: Boat

Expertise Rating: Novice

they have several distinguishing characteristics. Sea snakes have distinctive scales and a paddle-shaped tail. Eels lack scales, often have a long dorsal or ventral fin and have a gill opening at the back of the head. Though sea snakes are deadly poisonous, they are not aggressive toward people. You can observe them at very close range—just be careful not to touch!

Banded sea snakes are common at Ko Ha and, though poisonous, are not aggressive.

14 Ko Yung Pinnacle

Ko Yung Pinnacle is a small rock that reaches to within 6m of the surface. Because it is not always visible from the surface, only those who know the site well can find it. It's so rarely dived as to be virtually unknown, but when the conditions are right, it's one of the best dives around.

Location: north Ko Phi Phi Don, 4km (2.2 nautical miles) from Laem Tong

Depth Range: 6-36m (20-118ft)

Access: Boat

Expertise Rating: Advanced

The rocky pinnacle is one of the most luxuriant areas in all of Ko Phi Phi, completely covered with purple and pink soft corals. Down deep, large rays hide around the rocks at the base of the pinnacle. The gentle slope of the pinnacle itself is dotted with sea whips, many of which are more than 3m long. The pinnacle is also home to a very unusual type of black coral with pure-white polyps that make it look like a flocked Christmas tree, complete with ornamental oysters and crinoids.

Divers should take this site's advanced expertise rating seriously. Be extremely cautious here, as the currents can be nasty. Like all of Phi Phi Don's northern dive sites, visibility varies dramatically, but on good days, it can be more than 20m. When it's like that, it's magical.

MARK STRICKLAND

Delicate whip corals are common at Ko Yung Pinnacle.

Diving in Currents

Virtually all coral reefs with healthy, diverse marine life are subject to currents, at least some of the time. This relationship between rich marine life and currents is no coincidence: Most reef creatures rely on them in one way or another. But strong currents don't have to mean difficult diving, provided you utilize proper techniques.

Less Is More. While it is good to be prepared for the unexpected, streamline your gear by minimizing accessories that add bulk and increase drag. One essential item is a safety sausage, which can be inflated at the surface to make you more visible to boats: Always carry one when diving in open water.

Getting Down If the boat is secured to a mooring or anchor line, the best way to descend is by pulling hand over hand down the line. Don't start kicking until you reach the bottom, as this depletes your energy and air without providing any benefit.

Go with the Flow If the dive site is large and a current is running parallel to the reef, drift diving is the obvious way to go. By starting up-current, you can take in the scenery as you skim effortlessly over the reef. Be certain the crew is aware of your plans.

Use the Lay of the Land Underwater structures like rocks and coral heads can provide shelter from the current—even a half-meter-high rock will do a good job of this. Stay fairly close to the bottom and tuck behind such structures to find the "neutral areas." Be aware that currents are generally strongest at the top of these structures and in narrow valleys, which cause water to accelerate as it passes. While staying close to reef structures provides shelter from currents, be careful to avoid contact with delicate marine life.

Down-Currents Some sites are subject to downward flows that, though not necessarily dangerous, may prove a bit unsettling. Assuming that you have plenty of bottom time and air, it is often best to hold on to something (not live coral) and wait it out. Many down-currents last only a few minutes before reversing or dissipating. If the current shows no sign of letting up, try pulling yourself uphill by carefully grabbing dead coral, rocks or other nonliving reef structures. When moving against the current, be sure to pace your activity. If neither of the above techniques does the trick, you may need to abort the dive. Should this be necessary, let go of the reef, monitor your depth carefully and add air to your buoyancy compensator until you are no longer descending. Normally, the down-current will dissipate soon after you drift away from the reef. Because of this, there is a very real danger of an uncontrolled ascent as the added air expands inside your BC; be prepared to vent air out of your BC. Naturally, a lengthy safety stop is mandatory after a deep dive.

15 Ko Yung (Southeast Side)

Ko Yung's southeast side is a good site for novice divers, though it is not frequented by many dive shops due to its distance from port (Phi Phi Don's Tonsai Bay).

In general, the coral north of Phi Phi Don (toward Krabi) is less colorful than at other places along the coast, but there are still some interesting things to see here, often shallow enough for snorkelers to enjoy. The shallow parts of the reef are composed of staghorn coral, while lettuce corals predominate in deeper water.

Leopard sharks are very common at this dive site and, since they are unaccustomed to divers, are usually quite approachable. Urchins the size of your hand can cling easily and harmlessly to you with their suction-tube feet. Even

Location: North Ko Phi Phi Don, 4km (2.2 nautical miles) from Laem Tong

Depth Range: 2-18m (6.5-59ft)

Access: Boat

Expertise Rating: Novice

dolphins are seen on a regular basis, swimming close to shore in the small bay.

Be careful of the prevailing currents, as they can move you along the island at a quick pace. Make sure the boat captain is watching and following you. Visibility varies dramatically, but this can be a great dive away from the crowds to the south.

16 Hin Pae (Long Beach)

Hin Pae is one of Phi Phi's best snorkeling sites, and is also popular as a dive-training site. It's a 10-minute boat ride from Tonsai Bay, or a relatively long swim from Long Beach on the southeast coast of Ko Phi Phi Don.

The shallow hard-coral bommies are surrounded by sandy areas, and the reef slopes gently away from the shore—a fairly typical reef formation. You can find lots

Location: About 200m (650ft) west of Long Beach on Ko Phi Phi Don

Depth Range: 2-12m (6.5-40ft)

Access: Shore or boat

Expertise Rating: Intermediate

of critters in the shallows, and some of Ko Phi Phi's largest groupers reside here.

Snorkelers consistently see blacktip reef sharks here, which for the uninitiated can be a bit unsettling. Don't worry, these sharks are more interested in cruising the reef than bothering with divers or snorkelers. These sharks are rarely seen by divers, so when your tank is empty, snorkel a bit. It's the best way to see blacktip reef sharks around Ko Phi Phi.

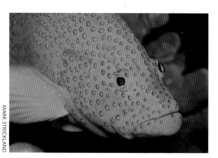

MARK STRICKLAND

Blue-spotted coral grouper live at Hin Pae.

17 Maya Cave

Ao Maya was the primary site in the film *The Beach*. The bay has not only a beautiful beach on the south part of the cove, but also excellent snorkeling over hard-coral bommies on its east and north sides, and it's big enough for several large boats to moor at concurrently.

Most divers who come here want to have a look at the southwest point, where they'll find Maya Cave, the biggest cave in the Ko Phi Phi area. Even if you are not a cave or cavern diver, you can get a taste for what this one is like just by swimming along the entrance, which is more than 20m wide.

Most dives start with a descent to about 20m just west of the bay's southwest point. The steep slope is covered with a variety of tropical fish, sea fans, sea whips and usually quite a few scorpion-

Location: Southwest of Ko Phi Phi Lae

Depth Range: 0-24m (0-79ft)

Access: Boat

Expertise Rating: Novice within the bay, Advanced to penetrate the cave

fish. If you plan to enter the cavern, spend only a few minutes investigating the slope before ascending to the cave mouth at about 8m.

The cave's interior is almost devoid of life, but there are some schools of bronze sweepers that hover above the sandy floor. The first large chamber narrows after about 40m, and the entrance is normally still visible from this point. This is

MARK STRICKLAND

Colorful reef fish flit about near soft corals.

where it's still technically a cavern dive. Once you swim underneath the small overhang and enter the next chamber, from which several passages lead into other chambers, the dive becomes a cave dive and you'll need the appropriate cave diving equipment and certification. As long as you stay in the first chamber, a cavern diver certification is all that is required.

Several of the high chambers within this cavern system reach above sea level. The chamber in the front part of the cavern is easily seen while diving. You can surface into the stalactite-covered room with ceilings almost 15m high, doff your regulator and breathe the constantly refreshed air. To exit, just swim toward the light. This is a safe yet fascinating dive for those who are cavern certified.

18 Ao Losama

Often done as a second dive after neighboring Ko Bida Nok, this site is around a small limestone island that sits in the middle of Ao Losama. It is a good place for beginners to practice wall diving and buoyancy skills, as the rocky island drops vertically to a sandy bottom at only 12m inside the cove and down to 22m on the eastern end of the island. Losama is a beautiful place for snorkelers too, with marine life all the way to the surface and plenty to see within free-diving depths. The rock is small enough to snorkel in less than an hour or dive on a single tank. Sea cucumbers and lush soft corals cling to its surface. Five species of anemonefish reside here, including the aggressive saddleback anemonefish, which may make a mad dash for your mask (and even bump into it occasionally).

Most divers descend on the eastern side of the rock, where you'll find a canyon at about 18m bordered by the island to the west and a ridge on the eastern side. Huge sea fans cover its walls. Large groupers sometimes hang out at either end of the canyon—if you're careful you may get a quick look before they dive for cover. The southern part of the rock has some gentle overhangs and depressions that block out the light,

Location: Southeast Ko Phi Phi Lae

Depth Range: 0-22m (0-72 ft)

Access: Boat

Expertise Rating: Novice

making you feel as if you're in an overhead environment.

Advanced divers may want to explore the western end of the cove, where there is a cave at about 18m. A large school of cobia fish (which look surprisingly like sharks) often congregates here.

MARK STRICKLAND
Red saddleback anemonefish, snuggling with its host anemone.

19 Ko Bida Nok

One of the most popular and scenic dive sites of the Phi Phi area is Ko Bida Nok. This small island—almost small enough to circumnavigate on one dive—rises vertically to about 45m above sea level. Below sea level, the island plunges just as steeply to almost 30m, providing divers with coral-covered walls, gentle currents and a variety of marine life to enjoy.

Location: South of Ko Phi Phi Lae

Depth Range: 0-33m (0-108ft)

Access: Boat

Expertise Rating: Intermediate

Dives usually start in a little cove on the east side of the island, where longtail boats can moor easily (larger vessels stay slightly outside of the bay), but entry points may vary depending on the direction of the wind and currents. After you enter the water, it's best to swim at the surface south and slightly east away from the cove until you can see coral beneath you. Descend and continue south-southeast to a nearly vertical wall, which you can follow down to its base at almost 28m. Just a few meters away and in slightly deeper water (30 to 33m), you'll find a rock covered with large orange sea fans, several colors of soft corals and, at most times of the year, a thick layer of silversides.

Return to the wall and allow the current to gently push you west. The nearly vertical wall transitions to a gentle slope, where you'll find many of the typical reef

MARK STRICKLAND

Octopuses often hide under Ko Bida Nok's ledges.

inhabitants of the Andaman Sea. Schools of bigeye snappers, anemones and their fish companions, sea whips and several species of lionfish are common. The sea fans are gorgeous and very healthy at this dive site. Octopuses often hide under several ledges that stick out from the main reef. If the visibility is good—and it is often as good as 25m here—keep an eye out for leopard sharks swimming along the wall or lying in the sand.

As you ascend at the end of the dive, look for a cavern at about 5m. It bends first to the right and then the left, and as you look up, you can see the sun shining through some cracks in the island.

Surfacing next to the island is very dramatic, but the surge and current can make floating at the surface rather dangerous. Be careful and swim away from the island after surfacing so the boat can pick you up safely.

20 Hin Bida

This large, exposed flat rock pierces the water's surface during all but the highest of tides. Its base at about 22m is surrounded by hard corals and boulders, and the seafloor becomes increasingly sandy as you move away from the rock. Start your dive over the sand, and use the current to your advantage by drift diving over the relatively shallow corals.

Location: 6km (3.2 nautical miles) southeast of Ko Bida Nok

Depth Range: 0-22m (0-75ft)

Access: Boat

Expertise Rating: Intermediate

Though the reef formations underwater aren't noteworthy, leopard sharks are often seen along the sandy seafloor, and black-spotted rays enjoy the protection offered by the boulders. Catch a glimpse of the damselfish that hover above the large patches of healthy staghorn coral, darting into the branches to hide as divers swim by.

MARK STRICKLAND

Blue-ringed angelfish are friendly, photogenic and common in Thailand.

Trang & Southern Dive Sites

The Trang dive region covers the coastal areas and islands south of Krabi Province, from Ko Lanta south to the port of Kantang and as far west as Hin Daeng (60km off the coast). The region's islands feature beautiful and varied topography, from craggy limestone cliffs to rolling hills covered by lush rainforest. The most famous island and also the largest is Ko Lanta, which is almost the same size as Phuket but with a very small population. Ko Lanta encompasses two islands—Ko Lanta Yai (*yai* meaning "larger") and Ko Lanta Noi (*noi* is the "smaller")—separated from each other and the mainland by narrow channels. Though not connected to the mainland by a bridge, car ferries cross the narrow channels in just a few minutes. It is also accessible by boat from Ko Phi Phi. There are few places to dive or snorkel around Ko Lanta, but it is one of the departure points for Trang daytrips.

Live-aboards from Phuket have been diving the Trang region since the early 1990s, but Trang has not kept pace with the tourism development of its northern neighbors. With its poor infrastructure and lack of English speakers, it will probably be a long time before the diving industry develops here to the extent it has in Ko Samui or Phuket. However, diving in the Trang region is easily accomplished via Phuket dive operators.

Though it doesn't have as many dive sites as other Andaman Coast regions, Trang's few world-class dive sites are definitely worth a visit. Two pinnacles—Hin Daeng (Red Rock) and Hin Muang (Purple Rock)—have done much to popularize Trang diving. They offer everything from dramatic walls and big fish action to lush underwater coral gardens—truly superlative diving. Other popular dive areas include Ko Ha, Ko Rok and the inshore areas of Ko Muk and Ko Ngai. Although you'll find many other islands and coastal areas that are beautiful topside, many

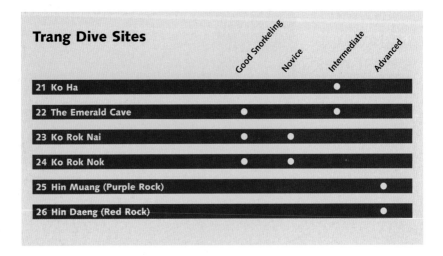

Trang Dive Sites	Good Snorkeling	Novice	Intermediate	Advanced
21 Ko Ha			●	
22 The Emerald Cave	●		●	
23 Ko Rok Nai	●	●		
24 Ko Rok Nok	●	●		
25 Hin Muang (Purple Rock)				●
26 Hin Daeng (Red Rock)				●

have problems with river runoff, which creates poor visibility and hinders the development of coral reefs.

Because of the remote dive site locations, most diving in the Trang area is via live-aboard vessels. The vast majority of these trips leave from Phuket, and a few boats depart from Ko Phi Phi as well. It is possible to visit a few of the sites by daytrip via speedboat from Ko Phi Phi or slower boats from Ko Lanta. Longtails are even used by some dive centers in Ko Lanta for trips to Ko Ha, but for trips to Hin Daeng, either a live-aboard or a speed boat is needed to access the site. Trips to the Emerald Cave or Ko Rok can be arranged from Ko Lanta, Trang City, the port at Kantang, Ko Muk or Ko Ngai.

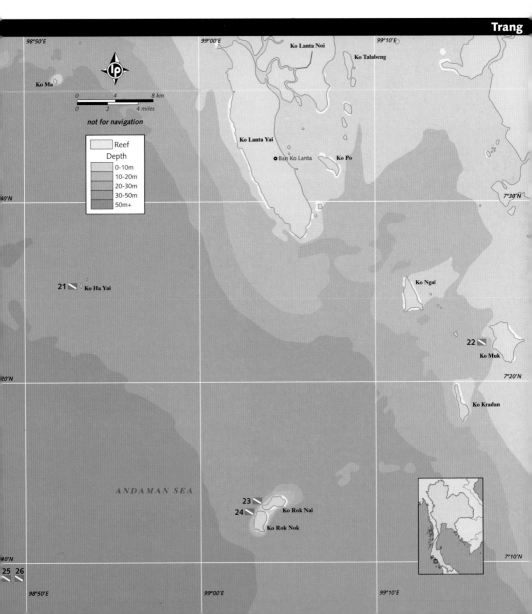

21 Ko Ha

Ko Ha is a cluster of five small islands (*ha* is Thai for five) 15km west-southwest of Ko Lanta's southern tip. These limestone islands are separated by channels more than 50m deep. Unlike Ko Phi Phi, the water here is ordinarily quite clear and visibility frequently exceeds 30m.

Location: 36km (20 nautical miles) south of Ko Phi Phi Don

Depth Range: 5-36m (16-118ft)

Access: Boat or live-aboard

Expertise Rating: Intermediate

Though there are dive sites at all of the islands, the most popular is **Ko Ha Yai,** the largest island and the farthest to the west. In good weather, the dive begins on the island's western side where you descend onto a sloping wall made up of corals and large smooth rocks. Descend to approximately 21m and swim south, following the curve of the reef. You'll pass a few small outcroppings and bommies with beautiful fans and sea whips, often surrounded by huge schools of translucent silverside fish. These bommies rise up from patches of pure-white sand. The reef slopes to beyond 50m, so be sure to look out into the blue water

for whale sharks, large tuna and jacks, as well as Japanese rays, black-spotted stingrays and mobula rays.

Moving up the slope into shallower water, you'll come to the dive site's highlights: two caverns whose entrances are at a depth of about 10m. These caverns are safe to enter, even without a light, as the entrances are large and there is only one way in and one way out of each cavern. The best part of these caves is that you can surface inside and view stalactites hanging down from the ceiling

MARK STRICKLAND

It is worth exploring Ko Ha Yai's underwater cavern during the day or night.

more than 30m overhead. The quality of light filtering through the water from the entrance is magical.

The caverns are a particularly beautiful place to visit at night because of the bioluminescent plankton. Turn off your dive light to marvel at the streaks and streams of light produced by these dynoflagellates, which emit a distinctive blue glow when disturbed. You may not be the only one enjoying the show: giant trevally have been seen trailing bioluminescent tracers as they crisscross the cavern, illuminated by the moonlight through the entrance.

At the bottom of the easternmost cavern you can access a narrow cave via a small aperture. Only one diver can enter at a time. This part of the dive should be attempted only by qualified cave divers using appropriate equipment. You can follow the passage for approximately 20m, where it dead-ends at a large chamber. Despite the fact that there is only one way in and out, light sand is easily kicked up, making disorientation a major problem. If this happens you could use your whole air supply trying the find the exit.

22   The Emerald Cave

Although the visibility around Ko Lanta's inshore islands is generally poor and many experienced divers find the reefs uninteresting, Ko Muk has one dive worth mentioning: Emerald Cave (*Tam Morakort* in Thai). Though it's not worth going out of your way for, it's definitely worth a visit if you're in the area.

You'll find the cavern on Ko Muk's northwest corner. At high tide, it's worth diving through the 30m long cavern, which leads to a *hong*. A hong is a large opening in the center of an island, kind of like the hole in a doughnut. Ko Muk's hong is surround by towering cliffs edged by a perfect little white-sand beach, behind which is a dense tropical forest. At extremely low tide the cavern is large enough for a longtail boat to maneuver through, or you can snorkel through to the hong, an especially nice activity for those staying on the island.

Midway through the main passage and on the left side, a side passage leads to a small cavern that has an air pocket you can surface in. As getting lost inside the cave is a definite possibility, having

Location: 20km (11 nautical miles) southeast of the southern tip of Ko Lanta

Depth Range: 2-12m (6.5-40ft)

Access: Boat

Expertise Rating: Intermediate

proper equipment and an experienced guide is a necessity except at extremely low tide, when you can swim safely along the surface without needing to descend.

Christmas tree worms come in a range of colors.

23 | Ko Rok Nai

Ko Rok Nai and Ko Rok Nok ("Inside" and "Outside" Islands) have some of the prettiest beaches in Thailand and are un-inhabited (except for a national park ranger station on Ko Rok Nai). They are also some of the most densely forested islands in the area, covered completely by huge hardwood trees. With a lot of patience and a bit of luck, you may see the islands' namesake onshore: The small, furry mammals (*rok*) resemble squirrels and can jump from tree to tree. But you are much more likely to see monitor lizards, which look similar to Indonesia's famous Komodo Dragons, but grow to only 1m.

The two sister islands are separated by a relatively narrow 15m deep channel. The best dive on Ko Rok Nai is on the northern coast starting in a small rocky cove. From here you can drift with the current along a shallow, beautiful and very diverse coral reef. You'll find many species of hard corals, but very few large

Location: 30km (16 nautical miles) south of Ko Lanta

Depth Range: 5-12m (16-40ft)

Access: Boat or live-aboard

Expertise Rating: Novice

fans or soft corals. For some reason, the corals are not as brightly colored here as they are elsewhere in the Andaman Sea. Despite this, the fish life is absolutely fantastic and less shy than at other sites. Large schools of bigeye snappers hover over the coral, and this is one place where you may see a few huge groupers.

Look closely under crevices and over-hangs to see the occasional seahorse, as well as frogfish and other unusual animals. This is also one of the best places to see giant clams, or *Tridacnas*, which are fairly uncommon in Thailand. Though not as big as the Australian variety, their striking patterns are every bit as colorful.

With the site's deepest point at about 12m, it's a beautiful, relaxing shallow dive that is safer and more interesting than a third dive at Hin Daeng. This is also a good snorkeling site, though some free-diving is necessary since visibility is often less than 12m and the good coral growth begins at about 5m. There are other sites along the northeast side of the island that are better for snorkeling.

MARK STRICKLAND
Giant clams are more common at Ko Rok Nai than nearly any other Thai site.

24 Ko Rok Nok

There are several dive sites around Ko Rok Nok, but probably the best is right at the western entrance to the channel that separates the islands. It's not a particularly dramatic reef so advanced divers may tire of it quickly, but if you take your time and look closely there can be some nice surprises.

Location: 30km (16 nautical miles) south of Ko Lanta

Depth Range: 5-23 m (16-75ft)

Access: Boat or live-aboard

Expertise Rating: Novice

When the current is flowing north to south (its typical course), it's best to begin the dive at the northern tip of the island's cape. As you descend, the current will help push you around to the south so that you can continue your dive parallel to the island along it's west side. There is normally enough current here for a one-way drift dive.

The dive is relatively shallow, with the best corals and fish life above 18m. The bottom is composed of hard corals, with a sprinkling of soft coral in deeper areas. Blacktip sharks patrol the reef shallows and hawksbill turtles are seen regularly. Though the marine life is not as abundant as at other places along the coast, if you are diving in the region and it's too windy to make the trip out to Hin Daeng, it's worth jumping in here. For novice divers, this site is much easier than the pinnacles to the west.

On the island, a curious driftwood shrine carved by local fishermen pays homage to a particular part of the male anatomy: It is covered with more than 100 phallic symbols. If diving conditions don't cooperate, the short walk to this shrine makes for a nice shore excursion.

Hawksbill turtles are seen regularly at Ko Rok Nok.

25 Hin Muang (Purple Rock)

Hin Muang is a long, rocky ridge that lies just a few hundred meters northeast of Hin Daeng. The pinnacle itself is approximately 200m long and less than 30m wide, and is shaped like an immense loaf of bread with its rounded top at 8m and its steep, vertical sides dropping below recreational diving limits. This ridge is connected to Hin Daeng, but as most of it tops out below 30m, it is usually too far to dive from one reef to the other without exceeding no-decompression limits. However, when a good current is running from west to east, it is quite feasible to make the swim in 12 to 15 minutes, allowing you to ascend and off-gas at the shallow portions of Hin Daeng.

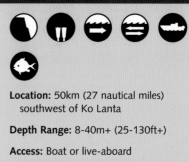

Location: 50km (27 nautical miles) southwest of Ko Lanta

Depth Range: 8-40m+ (25-130ft+)

Access: Boat or live-aboard

Expertise Rating: Advanced

The first time you dive Hin Muang, you may be surprised at the incredible amount of marine life that clings to this reef. It is as if the rock is in another ocean and not just a short distance away from the relatively barren Hin Daeng. The name (Purple Rock) is derived from the thick growths of purple soft corals that cover nearly every available surface below 15m. Actually a deep red color, these delicate filter feeders appear purple at depth. Clouds of glassfish (also called silversides) school around the fans and rocky outcroppings. Carpets of anemones cover the shallower sections of the pinnacle.

Cuttlefish are fairly common and often display a rainbow of colors while courting. Leopard sharks like to hang out at a sandy plateau at 30m, just east of the reef crest. Lionfish seem to be everywhere and are very approachable, making most underwater photographers very happy indeed.

Whale sharks have been seen repeatedly around these pinnacles. For many years, Hin Muang was known as *the* place to spot them, but their numbers vary from year to year. These docile creatures often allow divers to get quite close, but don't take this as an invitation to touch them. If you do they are likely to swim away.

You may also have the chance to swim with grey reef sharks in the deep blue water off Hin Daeng or Hin Muang. Although shark identification is difficult, grey reef sharks are relatively easy to distinguish by the black vertical stripe along their caudal, or tail, fin. These sharks are usually seen in groups—sometimes 10 or more at a time—in the blue water off these pinnacles. These sharks do not have a reputation for aggressiveness, but it pays to be cautious. Instead of approaching the sharks, wait for them to approach you.

Even without the large-animal sightings, Hin Muang is a wonderful dive site. This area offers some of the best visibility in the Andaman Sea when the conditions are right. The sheer drama of diving on such a large pinnacle, as well as the variety of marine life found here, makes it a dive worth repeating.

MARK STRICKLAND

Hin Muang's soft corals make colorful photo subjects.

26 Hin Daeng (Red Rock)

Although Hin Daeng looks insignificant from the surface, underwater the rock is mammoth. For those of you who love wall diving, this is Thailand's best.

The southern side descends almost straight down to beyond 60m, forming the most radical vertical drop in Thailand's seas. This wall is dotted with light growths of soft corals and a few sea fans and black corals, but is otherwise not very interesting as far as marine life goes—other areas of the site have better coral growth. Occasional schools of grey reef sharks patrol this area, as do mantas, whale sharks and other large fish, including leopard sharks, which are often found on the deeper ledges here.

On the eastern side where the slope is more gentle, two long ridges descend into the blue. When the currents are favorable, you can follow these ridges down to 40m or more—just be careful of the long return swim. Here the soft coral is lush and tall. Huge schools of jacks sometimes sweep past the ridge, surrounding divers in a shimmering cloud of silver.

Along the western face of the pinnacle, you will find several canyons, one of which is densely carpeted with anemones. The northern area slopes gently to a sandy bottom. The rocks along the slope form nooks and crannies for several species of eels to hide in, including some healthy giant morays. Large stingrays hug the bottom as they hunt for food.

In shallower areas, a school of friendly batfish may greet you as you make your way up the slope. Octopuses and cuttlefish are also relatively common, as are sea cucumbers, anemones and lots of long-spine sea urchins. During your safety

Location: 50km (27 nautical miles) southwest of Ko Lanta

Depth Range: 0-40m+ (0-130ft+)

Access: Boat or live-aboard

Expertise Rating: Advanced

stop, check out the vertical rock surfaces for nudibranchs; there are often several species browsing in the shallows.

The quality of the diving at Hin Daeng varies from year to year—some years there are amazing amounts of marine life, and at other times there is not much to see at all. Shark activity also varies dramatically, and seems to be declining. This may be due to the increasing number of divers visiting the site, environmental changes or overfishing, though the reasons are not clear. Although the pinnacle is always impressive due to its canyons and vertical walls, seeing a lot of fish makes the dive much more enjoyable.

As strong currents are often present, Hin Daeng can be a challenging dive. Also be careful of the depths, as it's quite easy to exceed 30m at almost any point on the rock. If you find yourself at the bottom you're way too deep! Finally, when surfacing, ascend away from the exposed rock on the surface. If you get too close the surge may wash you against it, and the boat will not be able to pick you up easily. The shallow area near the rock island is a nice place to do a safety stop, but during the last couple of minutes let the current take you over deeper water.

Southern Dive Sites

Satun, the southernmost province on Thailand's Andaman Coast, is the gateway to Ko Tarutao. Still largely unspoiled, this lush, mountainous island became Thailand's first Marine National Park in 1974. The park consists of 51 islands and many coral reefs that offer considerable potential for snorkeling and diving. Presently, however, there are surprisingly few options for dedicated dive trips, due in part to logistics; Satun is a long way from the Phuket and Krabi resort areas, and getting to the outer islands is not always easy.

Though some reefs have been damaged by blast fishing and crown-of-thorns sea stars, a handful of locations worth diving are listed below. In spite of being the best-known island and the namesake for the national park, Ko Tarutao is not included. While there are areas of good coral growth at Tarutao, it is too close to shore to offer good visibility. The best diving, in terms of both marine life and visibility, tends to be farther offshore, where you'll find an abundance of pristine hard and soft corals, prolific fish life and a wide variety of invertebrates. Sharks and rays are also seen regularly, due in part to the lack of divers.

Ko Sawang's east end offers good soft coral, healthy fish life and a chance to see eagle rays and whitetip reef sharks. Underwater terrain is rocky, stepping from 9m to a sandy bottom at 24m. Another recommended site is **Ko Hin Son**, a series of shallow rocks that breaks the surface just south of a navigational beacon, between Ko Sawang and Ko Palai. You'll find good soft coral and a wealth of small critters at around 10 to 12m. Hard corals are more prevalent in the shallower depths. Between Ko Bulo and Ko Adang is **Hin Ja Bang** (Arch Rock), where healthy soft coral and lots of colorful fish are found between 4 and 10m. Farther north, about halfway between Ko Rawi and Ko Adang, **Ko Kata** makes a good night dive with plenty of hard and soft corals, small fish and lots of interesting invertebrates. From the two moorings (in 10 to 12m) on the island's south side, follow the sloping bottom down to about 18m. The sites described above are only a sample of what the area has to offer; as the area is explored more extensively additional dive sites will likely be discovered.

This area offers snorkelers many healthy, shallow coral reefs. Since snorkeling doesn't require the equipment and infrastructure of scuba diving, it is perhaps the ideal way to explore the region's many reefs. **Ko Kata** (Ko Yang) and **Ko Bulo** (Ko Hing Ngam) are especially good snorkeling sites. There are also shallow reefs around **Mu Ko Klang** (a cluster of three small islands roughly halfway between Ko Tarutao and the Ko Adang/Rawi group).

None of these islands is easily accessible during the rainy season, but from November through mid-April, boats depart daily from Pak Bara (a small village about 60km northwest of Satun) for Ko Tarutao, Ko Adang and Ko Lipe. Ko Lipe is the main place to stay in the islands, and has a wide range of accommodations and restaurants. There are also basic accommodations and limited food options on Ko Tarutao and Ko Adang. Sailing yachts also frequently stop by on the popular run from Phuket to Langkawi in Malaysia. As of this writing, only Professional Diver Co. offers semi-regular trips on the live-aboard *ScubaNet*. For more information, contact ☎ (2) 954 0010 or 0011 fax: (2) 954 0552, email: prodive1@ksc.th.com, or www.prodive.th.com.

MARK STRICKLAND

Red-bar anthias add brilliant splashes of color to certain sites in the Ko Adang and Butang areas.

Similan Islands Dive Sites

Blessed with some of Thailand's healthiest and most diverse reefs, the Similan Islands National Marine Park is widely recognized as one of the kingdom's top dive locales. Located 95 to 114km (50 to 60 nautical miles) from Phuket and roughly 72km (38 nautical miles) from the mainland, the Similans consist of nine relatively small islands and their surrounding reefs. In fact, the name Similan is thought to have originated from the Malaysian word *sembelan*, meaning nine. Most of these islands have Thai names, but even Thai fishermen refer to them "by the numbers,"

Similan Islands Dive Sites

	Good Snorkeling	Novice	Intermediate	Advanced
27 Eastern Shallows	●		●	
28 Rocky Point			●	
29 Coral Gardens	●	●		
30 Boulder City			●	
31 Shark Fin Reef (Hin Pae)			●	
32 Stonehenge			●	
33 East of Eden	●		●	
34 Fanfare Point			●	
35 Elephant's Head (Hin Pusar)	●		●	
36 Beacon Beach South (Beacon Point)	●		●	
37 Beacon Beach	●	●		
38 Fantasea Reef				●
39 Turtle Rock	●		●	
40 Donald Duck Bay	●	●		
41 Snapper Alley			●	
42 The Hideaway	●		●	
43 Bommies			●	
44 Christmas Point	●		●	

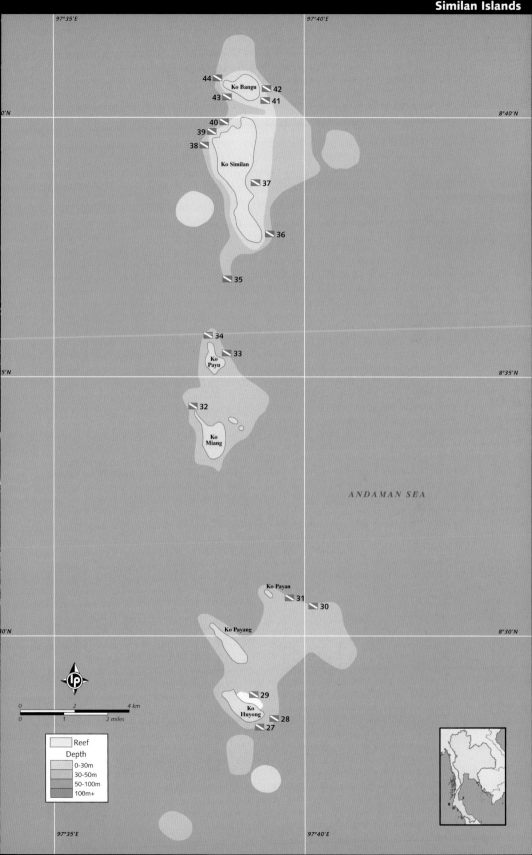

starting with #1 at the south end and culminating with #9 at the north. Strung across about 19km (10 nautical miles), most of the Similans are uninhabited (#4 hosts the park headquarters, and a small ranger station is on #8). The islands themselves are rugged and beautiful, composed primarily of granite rocks and dense vegetation. While shorelines of the smaller islands are mostly rocky, the larger ones feature some of the finest beaches anywhere.

Underwater, the terrain and marine life vary depending on which side of the island chain you are diving. At most east-facing sites, gentle currents and generally easy diving conditions prevail, with white-sand bottoms and sloping, predominantly hard-coral reefs. Fish life is prolific and diverse, with an abundance of colorful reef species like angelfish, butterflyfish, damselfish, anthias and many others.

Less than a mile away, west-facing sites are very different, with piles of huge granite boulders creating dramatic, high-profile formations. Many sites feature intriguing archways, tunnels and swim-throughs, and most offer impressive scenic vistas. Currents on the west side tend to be unpredictable, at times creating conditions that may prove challenging for inexperienced divers. Frequently, turbulent clouds of cold, green water pass over certain reefs, temporarily reducing both temperature and visibility. However, these upwellings seldom last more than a few minutes, and they provide a rich supply of nutrients that supports dense populations of soft corals, gorgonians, crinoids and other filter feeders.

Because of the remote location, almost all diving in the Similans is via liveaboard vessels. The vast majority of these trips leave from Phuket, although a few boats also depart from Ko Phi Phi, Thap Lamu and Khao Lak National Park. If you don't have time for a live-aboard trip, you can visit the Similans on a daytrip, but with up to 222km (120 nautical miles) to cover round-trip from Phuket, you'll spend more time traveling than experiencing the islands. Daytrips are normally available only during the high season (December through early April).

This lush, granite island chain provides a beautiful backdrop for a day of snorkeling or diving.

27 | Eastern Shallows

While the entire perimeter of Similan #1 has at least some coral growth, you'll find the small section on the southwest side of the southeast tip to be some of the best. In this area, a nearly pristine hard-coral reef slopes gradually from safety-stop depth to 24m or so, where it meets a white-sand bottom. While not a large area, this site is one of the healthiest reefs in the Simi-lans, with many varieties of stony coral and occasional soft corals.

Location: South tip of Similan #1 (Ko Huyong)

Depth Range: 3-24m (10-79ft)

Access: Live-aboard

Expertise Rating: Intermediate

The wide range of reef fish found here includes blue-spotted groupers and Indian flame basslets at depth, and schools of convict surgeonfish and various parrotfish in the shallows. This area also offers excellent snorkeling, with large, intact coral colonies and an abundance of colorful reef fish in depths as shallow as 3m.

MARK STRICKLAND

Convict surgeonfish school over staghorn coral.

28 | Rocky Point

This site consists of a submerged ridge of granite just beyond the easternmost point of Similan #1. Normally there is a mooring attached at a depth of about 15m near the western end of this reef.

Bathed by vigorous currents, this reef supports healthy growths of crinoids and soft corals in certain areas. As with most sites in the Similans, it is worth having a look among the many rocky crevices, where several species of crabs, shrimp and small fish often gather.

Location: Southeast tip of Similan #1 (Ko Huyong)

Depth Range: 12-39m (40-128ft)

Access: Live-aboard

Expertise Rating: Intermediate

By and large, this is not an overly scenic site, but it can be a good place to encounter mid-water predators like dog-tooth tuna and various species of jacks, as well as bottom dwellers like blue-spotted and Jenkins stingrays, leopard sharks and occasional whitetip reef sharks.

Blue-spotted stringrays are a solitary species often found resting in deeper water (usually below 30m) along sandy bottoms near rocky or coral reefs. They can grow to 70cm long, excluding their tail. The venomous spine on their tail can inflict a painful wound, but they are not apt to use it unless they are stepped on or otherwise bothered.

Stingrays are sometimes encountered resting on the sandy bottom, usually below 30m.

29 Coral Gardens

Another good diving and snorkeling site, Coral Gardens is a large fringing reef that runs parallel to Similan #1's north-facing beach, which is the longest and arguably most beautiful beach in the Similans.

This site is aptly named, with a wide assortment of hard corals, including patches of staghorn and large boulder corals. Regrettably, many of these corals were eaten during a crown-of-thorns sea star invasion in the early 1990s, but new growths have started to take hold in many areas. Starting in water so shallow that corals are exposed at low tide, the reef gradually slopes down to a white-sand bottom at 18 to 24m. While hard corals are the main feature, some of the deeper bommies also support impressive soft corals, which thrive in the moderate

Location: North side of Similan #1 (Ko Huyong)

Depth Range: 1-24m (3.3-79ft)

Access: Live-aboard

Expertise Rating: Novice

current that runs parallel to the reef much of the time. Look for a sampling of colorful reef fish, as well as blue-spotted rays and lizardfish, both of which are experts at blending in with the sand bottom. Also abundant in sandy areas are shy garden eels, looking very much like a field of grass that recedes into the sand as you approach.

30 Boulder City

Boulder City is a distant part of the same ridge that makes up neighboring Shark Fin Reef. It covers a fairly large area, normally requiring two dives to see the entire site. As the name implies, granite boulders are a prominent feature, complemented by numerous large sea fans and scattered hard corals.

Investigate the reef's perimeter between 24 and 30m, where you'll almost certainly see blue-spotted rays resting in the sand and, possibly, leopard sharks. While not especially common, other big fish—like bumphead parrotfish, Napoleon wrasse and mantas—are seen here with higher frequency than at most sites in the area. A wide range of other creatures call this site home, including common lionfish, which sometimes gather in large numbers to herd baitfish among the fan corals. As air supply and bottom time dictate, move toward shallower areas at the center of the site, where two parallel rock ridges rise to 12m. While barren in some areas, several crevices

Location: 3km (1.6 nautical miles) southeast of Similan #3 (Ko Payan)

Depth Range: 12-33m (40-108ft)

Access: Live-aboard

Expertise Rating: Intermediate

provide homes for giant morays, spotfin lionfish and clouds of jewel basslets.

MARK STRICKLAND

Sea fans are a colorful backdrop for reef bannerfish.

31 Shark Fin Reef (Hin Pae)

Southeast of Similan #3, this reef actually encompasses two different sites, one on each end of a long, rocky ridge that runs roughly southeast-northwest. The site's namesake—a narrow section of this rock ridge—is said to resemble a shark's fin where it pierces the surface.

Huge granite boulders dominate the southeastern end, forming several interesting swim-throughs and archways. At the northwestern end, the reef looks quite different: it is covered with an

Location: 1.6km (.87 nautical miles) southeast of Similan #3 (Ko Payan)

Depth Range: 0-30m (0-98ft)

Access: Live-aboard

Expertise Rating: Intermediate

assortment of hard corals, including large fields of staghorn and sizable mountain-coral bommies, especially on the north side of the ridge. Large fan corals populate many of the deeper areas, often surrounded by clouds of glassfish. Many other reef fish gather here as well, including an occasional Napoleon wrasse. Shark Fin is well suited as a multilevel dive, with interesting scenery extending from 30m up to safety-stop depth.

32 Stonehenge

Lying in open water in the pass between islands #4 and #7 (Ko Miang and Ko Payu), this is a fairly deep site—its shallowest features are at 18m. Underwater terrain is relatively level, with large boulders strewn over a white-sand bottom at an average depth of 27 to 30m.

Like its namesake in England, this site's megalithic boulders conjure up a sense of the unexpected: You might encounter almost any sort of marine life here. Divers see whitetip reef sharks and large stingrays with fair frequency, as well as turtles and schooling fish like jacks and pinjalo snappers. Amid

Location: Roughly 300m (1,000ft) north of Similan #4 (Ko Miang)

Depth Range: 18-36m (59-118ft)

Access: Live-aboard

Expertise Rating: Intermediate

the rocks, deep crevices provide shelter for shy creatures like soldierfish, sweetlips and spiny lobsters. Healthy fan corals, black corals and large barrel sponges also grow here.

Be Gentle with the Giant

MARK STRICKLAND

Giant barrel sponges are normally found at depths below 12m (40ft). The largest specimens typically occur in deep water along the forward slope of a reef. They can grow to more than 2m (6ft) high with an equal diameter.

Divers are often tempted to enter these large sponges. Barrel sponges grow only 2cm (1 inch) per year—a sponge large enough for a diver to enter may be more than 100 years old. Handling and entry of barrel sponges is discouraged because the lip breaks easily, disrupting the flow of water and food to the organism. Breakage also allows the entry of organisms that can weaken the sponge, which may even cause the colony's death.

33 East of Eden

East of Eden is a fairly compact site, yet offers some of the most beautiful underwater scenery found anywhere in the Similans. Bordering the easternmost point of Similan #7, this reef is subject to more current flow than most of the Similans' eastern sites. The site combines the best of both sides of the islands, blending the fragile beauty of a hard-coral reef with an abundance of colorful filter feeders. All of this, surrounded by a white-sand bottom, creates the impression of swimming in a giant aquarium.

Among the most scenic areas is the bottom of the slope between 30 and 36m, where huge fan corals and prolific soft corals adorn the seascape, along with schools of bigeyes and bluestriped snappers. While most divers concentrate on the general scenery, this is also

Location: East side of Similan #7 (Ko Payu)

Depth Range: 3-36m (10-118ft)

Access: Live-aboard

Expertise Rating: Intermediate

a great area for small critters like purple fire gobies, nudibranchs and well camouflaged allied cowries found hiding amid the branches of gorgonian fans. Superb scenery extends all the way up to safety-stop depth, where schools of yellow damselfish and orange anthias surround several massive coral bommies covered with soft corals and crinoids.

MARK STRICKLAND

A dinghy waits to pick up divers at East of Eden.

34 Fanfare Point

This rocky point off Similan #7's north tip offers both interesting topography and excellent marine life. It is worth going fairly deep here, from 30 to 42m, as this is where you'll find the site's best features. At this depth, the large barrel sponges and fan corals that cling to the rocky substrate provide cover for coral trout, lionfish and schools of baitfish.

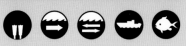

Location: North tip of Similan #7 (Ko Payu)

Depth Range: 5-40m+ (16-130ft+)

Access: Live-aboard

Expertise Rating: Intermediate

Linckia multiflora sea stars reproduce by dropping an arm that then "sprouts" more arms.

While marine life is not as lush in the shallower regions, this is still a good multilevel dive, with plenty of fish life as well as several interesting passageways through the rocks. A special "feature creature" of the shallows here is the *Linckia multiflora*, a mottled red, blue, yellow and white sea star that can grow to 6cm. They reproduce by periodically dropping off an arm, which then sprouts more arms to become a completely new animal. Look for them clinging to rocks between 6 and 15m.

35 Elephant's Head (Hin Pusar)

Considered by many to be the most spectacular site in the Similans, Elephant's Head features huge granite rocks that loom up from depths of more than 40m. Reaching well above the surface in several places, they are said to resemble the head and back of an elephant. These boulders form a complex series of archways and tunnels, all of which are easily navigated without special training or equipment.

Many of the rock surfaces are covered by lush growths of soft corals, sea fans and hard corals, which in turn

Location: Between Similan #7 (Ko Payu) and Similan #8 (Ko Similan)

Depth Range: 5-36m (16-118ft)

Access: Live-aboard

Expertise Rating: Intermediate

provide shelter for a wide spectrum of reef fish. This site is also a great place for small critters—it is worth looking around amid the coral gravel at 27m for nudibranchs, jawfish and at least two species of mantis shrimp. Take your time when exploring this rubble area, and you will have a good chance of finding flagtail gobies sitting outside the burrow they share with colorful Randall's shrimp.

Safety stops can also be rewarding if you scrutinize the shallow portions of the vertical rocks. You are almost certain to find "purple dragon" nudibranchs clinging to the wall, along with tiny hermit crabs and blennies that peer from old barnacles and worm holes. Not all the creatures here are miniscule—whitetip reef sharks are frequently encountered, especially on the north side.

MARK STRICKLAND

A diver's light reveals the soft coral's brilliant colors.

36 Beacon Beach South (Beacon Point)

Less than a kilometer south of Beacon Beach proper, this east-facing reef is just a continuation of the lengthy sloping dropoff that runs parallel to Similan #8. Although very similar to Beacon Beach, this site differs in one dramatic way—the coral here is much better.

A perfect multilevel dive, you can see great things at every depth here, from the deeper edges at 33 to 36m to the shallow reeftop at 5m or less. You'll find abundant and healthy hard corals along both the shallow reeftop and the steeply sloping drop-off. Fish life is also prolific. Divers have a good chance of encountering stingrays, which often rest in the white sand at the base of the slope.

Location: Southeast end of Similan #8 (Ko Similan)

Depth Range: 5-36m (16-118ft)

Access: Live-aboard

Expertise Rating: Intermediate

Often, a moderate current flows parallel to the shoreline, providing a free ride along this extensive reef. Just take care not to drift around the corner, where the rocky tip of the island could block the view that boat crews need to relocate divers on the surface.

37 Beacon Beach

Named for the navigational beacon that stands on a rocky ridge at the top of Similan #8, Beacon Beach is a steeply sloping, hard-coral reef that runs more or less parallel to the entire east coast of the island. While the reef here is not as scenic as at other sites, there are plenty of colorful fish, as well as a variety of corals and other invertebrates.

In shallow areas, mountain, staghorn and fire corals are scattered over much of the seafloor, while lettuce, honeycomb and bubble corals predominate in deeper zones. Unfortunately, several years ago a crown-of-thorns sea star invasion killed many of these, but there is still a fair amount of live coral. Nudibranchs, crinoids and pillow stars are common at most any depth.

Location: East side of Similan #8 (Ko Similan)

Depth Range: 6-30m (20-98ft)

Access: Live-aboard

Expertise Rating: Novice

You're likely to find many reef fish varieties here as well, including trumpetfish, pufferfish, goatfish, damselfish and many species of wrasse. Watch for freckled hawkfish perched amid coral branches, where they wait in ambush for unsuspecting shrimp and small fish.

Perhaps the biggest attraction of Beacon Beach, however, is its suitability as a checkout site. This is where many divers get their first underwater look at the Similans. While many areas have reasonably good coral growth, the shallow intermittent sand patches make this site an excellent choice for the first dive of a trip. By starting in such an area, you have a chance to sort out any buoyancy problems and make necessary adjustments without endangering delicate corals on the reef slope. This site also makes a good choice for night diving, with moderate depths and generally easy conditions.

MARK STRICKLAND

An overabundance of crown-of-thorns sea stars can destroy coral.

38 Fantasea Reef

Fantasea Reef offers everything found at the best west-side locations, including bold topography, caverns, swim-throughs and excellent gorgonians and soft corals. You will also find a proliferation of critters, including nudibranchs and mantis shrimp, typically around the deeper edges of the reef.

Location: Northwest end of Similan #8 (Ko Similan)

Depth Range: 6-40m+ (20-130ft+)

Access: Live-aboard

Expertise Rating: Advanced

It is the fish life, however, that really sets this place apart. Not only are fish found in great abundance and variety, they also seem much friendlier than at other sites. Here, normally shy species like butterflyfish and clown triggerfish act virtually unconcerned about divers, allowing for great photo opportunities.

Among the most photogenic residents are the blue-spotted coral groupers, which seem almost eager to pose for pictures. Other frequently seen species include unicornfish, lionfish, oriental and Andaman sweetlips, black snappers, giant morays and at least six species of angelfish. A few of the site's resident fish species are seldom seen elsewhere in the region, such as ribbon eels, purple fire gobies and bright-blue palette surgeonfish. Open-water predators like jacks, mackerel and dogtooth tuna make regular patrols here as well, often charging through schools of baitfish hovering near the reef. If the current is running, have a look around the up-current areas, as large schools of bannerfish and surgeonfish often congregate in mid-water.

Strong currents are quite common. Drift diving doesn't work well, because like most Thai reefs, the site is not large enough to allow more than a five-minute drift. Luckily, many high-profile boulders break up the current, creating areas that remain virtually current free. If the

MARK STRICKLAND

Diver looks through a natural porthole at Fantasea Reef.

current is just too strong, consider an alternative site and return an hour or two later when the current has lessened.

39 Turtle Rock

This fringing reef at the southwest corner of Donald Duck Bay is a good choice for an easy, convenient dive. While the bay's entire southern shoreline offers good diving, one of the best areas is beneath the turtle-shaped rock that gives this site its name. Here, granite boulders slope steeply down to a sand bottom. In deeper areas, between 21 and 30m, vibrant soft corals are common, while large fields of staghorn and other hard corals prevail in more-moderate depths. Fish life is abundant, with a good chance of encountering blue-ringed angelfish, coral trout and many other reef species.

Location: Northwest side of Similan #8 (Ko Similan)

Depth Range: 9-30m (30-98ft)

Access: Live-aboard

Expertise Rating: Intermediate

An especially interesting feature of this and other reefs in the area is the constant hum of fish activity around branching table (*Acropora*) corals. Often, dozens of damselfish call these places home, hovering over the formation until a threatening fish or diver comes too close. When this happens, the damselfish dive down amid the protective coral branches, peeking out occasionally to see if the coast is clear. These table corals are also favorite hangouts for brilliantly colored longnose filefish, which use their long snouts to reach down amid the branches for food.

40 Donald Duck Bay

Also known as Campbell's Bay or M-16 Bay, this site is perhaps best described by its Thai name, Ao Guak or "Shoe Bay," which refers to the shape of a prominent topside rock on the bay's north side. Featuring a beautiful white-sand beach backed by dense vegetation and rocks, this picturesque bay is among the most popular anchorages in the Similans.

Location: Northwest side of Similan #8 (Ko Similan)

Depth Range: 5-12m (16-40ft)

Access: Live-aboard

Expertise Rating: Novice

A trip ashore here is well worthwhile. You can easily climb to the "balancing rock," which offers spectacular views of the surrounding area. Another interesting attraction is the intact skeleton of a sperm whale that washed ashore several years ago: It is now reconstructed and nicely displayed at the ranger station just behind the beach.

Most divers don't consider this a prime dive site, yet it is still very popular for both divers and snorkelers because of the easy diving conditions and proximity to overnight boat moorings. While much of the coral is damaged, you'll see a variety of fish, including wrasse, surgeonfish, juvenile barracuda and several species of anemonefish. After dark, this site often proves to be surprisingly good, with a multitude of shrimp, morays and lionfish, as well as occasional sightings of cuttlefish.

Calm conditions make snorkeling a popular activity at Donald Duck Bay.

41 Snapper Alley

Snapper Alley is at the rocky southeast point of Similan #9, where granite boulders slope steeply down from the surface to a sand bottom at 30m or more.

Although the best diving is confined to a rather small area, the deeper rocks accommodate thriving soft corals, fragile green tubastraea and black-coral trees. Fish life is generally only fair, but may include blue-ringed angelfish, large pufferfish and possibly ribbon eels. As you work your way up to the shallows, be sure to check out the cavern at 6m, where you can spend your safety stop

Location: Southeast tip of Similan #9 (Ko Bangu)

Depth Range: 6-36m (20-118ft)

Access: Live-aboard

Expertise Rating: Intermediate

swimming amid snappers and other small fish. While conditions are usually easy here, currents can be very strong at times, so plan accordingly.

42 The Hideaway

Bordering the east side of Similan #9, this is another excellent multilevel site; you'll be captivated by the marine life from safety-stop depth all the way down the slope to 27m. Fish life is especially abundant, including blue-spotted groupers, bannerfish and painted sweetlips around the reef base, while the shallows are populated with colorful butterflyfish,

Location: East side of Similan #9 (Ko Bangu)

Depth Range: 5-27m (16-89ft)

Access: Live-aboard

Expertise Rating: Intermediate

regal angelfish and countless other species. This reef is especially active in early morning and late afternoon, when schools of snappers, queenfish and blue-fin trevallies charge through clouds of baitfish, gobbling up any that stray from the pack.

Although it consists primarily of hard coral, this site also has a few very healthy soft corals, gorgonians and black corals in

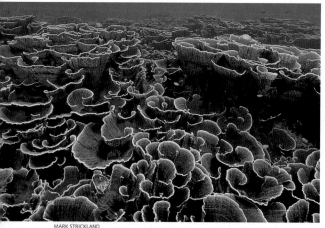

MARK STRICKLAND

This field of fine-pored coral is a hideaway for varied reef fish.

the deeper areas, mostly below 18m. In general, the best diving is on the slope itself, but if you swim a short distance over the sand to the east (away from the reef), you'll find several beautiful patch corals at about 27m.

Toward the end of your dive, allow some time to explore the shallows, which offer healthy hard corals and interesting creatures, as well as generally easy dive conditions. The Hideaway also has superb night diving with a wealth of invertebrates and fish life. Highlights include spiny lobsters, giant morays, large hermit crabs and lots of parrotfish sleeping amid the corals.

43 Bommies

The small cove on the south side of Similan #9 is an ideal place to seek shelter from the high season's prevailing northeast winds. While the entire cove offers enjoyable diving, by far the best area is a series of five large coral heads, or bommies, from which the site takes its name.

Scattered along a line that runs roughly east to west, these bommies are found anywhere between 18 and 21m deep, surrounded mostly by white sand. While the outer surfaces of the coral heads are interesting enough, the undersides are the real highlight: A profusion of sea fans and soft coral hangs down from the ceilings. While it may be tempting to swim under these structures, this is best avoided, as the delicate corals can be damaged easily.

Also a popular night dive, Bommies is a great place to look amid the sea fans and soft corals for

Location: South side of Similan #9 (Ko Bangu)

Depth Range: 18-24m (59-79ft)

Access: Live-aboard

Expertise Rating: Intermediate

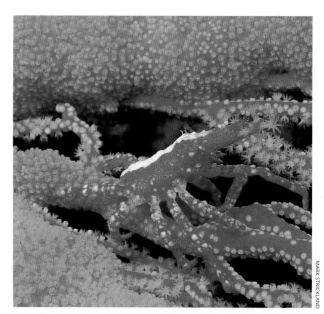

MARK STRICKLAND

This depressed gorgonian crab demonstrates its mastery of camouflage, looking nearly indistinguishable from its host.

small critters like dancing shrimp, spindle cowries and decorator crabs.

44 Christmas Point

Christmas Point is another typical west-side dive, boasting an extensive network of passageways and swim-throughs amid the rocky terrain. You can see virtually anything here, from soft corals and crinoids to whitetip reef sharks and occasional mantas. In particular, look for nudibranchs and mantis shrimp on the rubble bottom around the deeper edges of the reef.

This is also among the few places where divers consistently see egg cowries crawling on the leathery soft coral where they feed and spawn. Another highlight to watch for at this and other Similan sites is the cooperative feeding efforts of jacks, snappers and yellow-saddle goatfish. Terrorizing every small fish in their path, large mixed schools of these preda-

Location: Northwest side of Similan #9 (Ko Bangu)

Depth Range: 5-36m (16-118ft)

Access: Live-aboard

Expertise Rating: Intermediate

tors comb the reef, the goatfish using their chin barbels to flush out prey while the jacks and snappers mill around waiting to gobble up any stragglers.

Christmas Point is a perfect multilevel site, offering something of interest at every depth, even safety-stop depths, where ornamental boxfish and blue-lined surgeonfish browse in the surge zone.

MARK STRICKLAND

Soft corals inflate in the brisk current of Christmas Point.

Surin Dive Sites

The Surin region encompasses roughly 350 sq km (140 sq miles) of widely separated islands and reefs, including Ko Bon, Ko Tachai, the two main Surin Islands and their immediate neighbors, as well as Richelieu Rock, an isolated limestone pinnacle just 17km (9 nautical miles) east of Surin.

The physical characteristics of this region differ greatly from one area to the next, ranging from large granite islands to small limestone outcroppings. Underwater, the terrain is also highly varied, with fringing reefs, coral gardens, boulder formations and isolated pinnacles providing a wide range of habitats for a variety of marine life.

As with the Similan Islands, diver access to Surin is almost exclusively via live-aboard. Most leave from Phuket, though a few leave from Tap Lamu and Hat Kao Lak. For those who wish to stay in the simple bungalows at

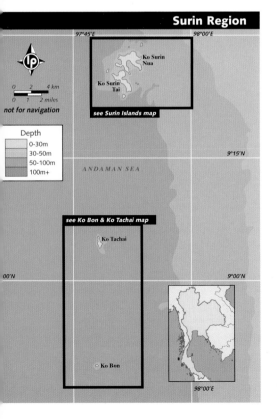

MARK STRICKLAND

Richelieu Rock is one of the best dive sites to see whale sharks.

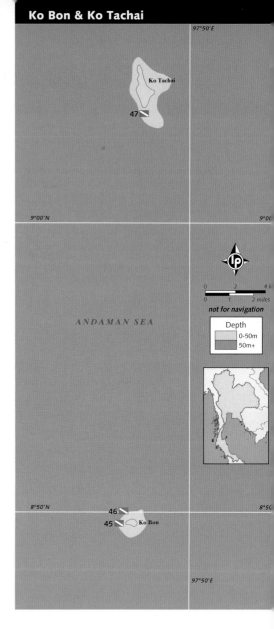

Ko Surin National Marine Park (snorkeling only), boats leave from the park office at the tiny village of Ngan Yong, about 6km (4 miles) north of Khuraburi. To check the boat schedule and bungalow availability, you can call the park office at ☎ (76) 491 378.

Ko Bon & Ko Tachai

Ko Bon and Ko Tachai are roughly 19km (10 nautical miles) apart and are far from both the Similan and Surin islands. Accordingly, they don't really belong to any particular island group. This book groups them with the Surin region for organizational purposes.

MARK STRICKLAND
Porcelain crab on adhesive anemone.

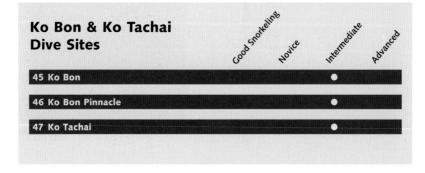

Ko Bon & Ko Tachai Dive Sites	Good Snorkeling	Novice	Intermediate	Advanced
45 Ko Bon			●	
46 Ko Bon Pinnacle			●	
47 Ko Tachai			●	

45 Ko Bon

Although it is visible from the Similans on a clear day, Ko Bon stands alone, both in terms of geography and geology (it is limestone, the Similans are granitic).

Above the waterline, this isolated island is an impressive sight, with steep rugged slopes and a tunnel running completely through it. Underwater, the main dive site is a narrow rocky ridge that slopes to below 42m off the south tip of the island. Much of this area is covered with small, vivid soft corals, which appear pastel blue at depth, but your dive light will reveal their true color—glowing pink. It is definitely worth exploring the deeper areas, where you'll frequently encounter leopard sharks, blue-spotted stingrays and marbled stingrays. Schools of jacks and snappers charge through the clouds of glassfish that hover around large fan corals and barrel sponges.

Although the best features are below 30m, shallower areas offer some interesting sights. On the west side of the point, damselfish, surgeonfish and wrasse populate the extensive fields of staghorn coral that cover the sloping bottom from 9 to 18m. The many crevices provide refuge for moray eels, squirrelfish and various species of puffers. Aside from the reef life, Ko Bon is also known as a good place to see big pelagic creatures—divers see

Location: 21km (11 nautical miles) north of the Similan Islands

Depth Range: 5-40m+ (15-130ft+)

Access: Live-aboard

Expertise Rating: Intermediate

mantas here quite regularly, along with occasional whale shark sightings.

One of the most interesting features of Ko Bon is a small hole in the rock wall, just above the waterline on the southwest point. When a swell is running, water cascades through this opening from the other side, creating clouds of bubbles that surge down to greet you during your safety stop.

MARK STRICKLAND

A diver is dwarfed by a large manta ray.

46 Ko Bon Pinnacle

This rock pinnacle lies well below the surface, reaching only 18m at its shallowest point and dropping to 39m or more at the base. The pinnacle itself supports a number of small, yellowish soft corals, as well as some nice gorgonian fans below 30m. Overall, however, the site lacks coral growth, and old fishing nets smother portions of the reef.

Despite the generally unimpressive scenery, this site can be worthwhile due to good schooling fish action; predators like bigeye jacks, rainbow runners and queenfish frequently patrol here. Plenty of plankton feeders hover nearby, including schools of batfish and large clouds of

Location: 21km (11 nautical miles) north of the Similan Islands

Depth Range: 18-40m+ (59-130ft+)

Access: Live-aboard

Expertise Rating: Intermediate

fusiliers. Blue-spotted and marbled stingrays frequently rest in the sand below 33m, as do leopard sharks. The pinnacle is among the best sites in the region for sighting mantas; whale sharks also make occasional appearances here.

Groomers of the Sea

Observant divers will discover a variety of symbiotic relationships—associations in which two dissimilar organisms participate in a mutually beneficial relationship—throughout the marine world. One of the most interesting is found at cleaning stations, where one animal advertises its grooming services to potential clients with a series of inviting undulating movements.

Cleaner species include gobies, wrasse, shrimp, angelfish, butterflyfish and tangs. One of the most common cleaners in Thailand is the blue-streak cleaner wrasse, a lively little fish that does a special "dance" to advertise its cleaning services. Once a fish makes the appropriate signals to be cleaned, the wrasse cleans debris, decaying skin and infection from all available surfaces, including the inside of a customer's mouth and gills. When danger approaches, the fish will close its mouth and gills, but still leave enough room for the wrasse to exit the much larger fish and retreat to safety. Although the customer could have

MARK STRICKLAND

an easy snack, it would never swallow the essential cleaner. The large fish benefits from the removal of parasites and dead tissue, while the little cleaner is provided with a "free" meal.

Divers will find that if they approach a cleaning station slowly and carefully, they'll be able to get closer to more fish than is normally possible and observe behavior seen nowhere else on the reef.

47 Ko Tachai

Roughly halfway between the Similan and the Surin island groups, the scenic Ko Tachai's elevated, rocky terrain is complemented by a spectacular white-sand beach on the north side.

Unfortunately, the shallow reef that borders this area has been heavily damaged by anchors and dynamite in years past and no longer qualifies as a prime dive site. However, on the island's south side there is an excellent reef consisting of a long ridge with a small pinnacle at its northern tip (nearest the island) and a large, dome-shaped structure on its south end. Known as **Twin Peaks**, this site is swept by nutrient-rich currents that nourish sea fans, whip corals, barrel sponges and other filter feeders, found particularly in deeper water.

This is also a good area to spot leopard sharks and stingrays, as well as trumpetfish, which are often seen try-

Location: 23km (12 nautical miles) north of Ko Bon

Depth Range: 12-36m (40-118ft)

Access: Live-aboard

Expertise Rating: Intermediate

ing to sneak up on prey by swimming piggyback over groupers or parrotfish. Dense mobs of schooling snappers and chevron barracuda are common. Hard corals and anemones are abundant, particularly in shallower depths.

Another highlight here is the prevalence of cleaning stations on top of the southern dome, especially amid the boulders near the mooring base, where long-finned batfish often line up to be serviced.

MARK STRICKLAND

Diver approaches giant sea fan at Ko Tachai.

The Surin Islands

Surin's two major islands, three smaller ones and several rocky islets are only a few kilometers south of the Myanmar border. This remote, sparsely inhabited area is part of the Thai national park system. The two main islands, Ko Surin Nua and Ko Surin Tai, are both breathtakingly beautiful. Their steep, rugged terrain is covered with an emerald green carpet of virgin jungle punctuated by towering ancient hardwoods.

Underwater, Surin boasts fringing reefs near the main islands as well as several offshore pinnacles and islets. The sloping reefs that line the main islands'

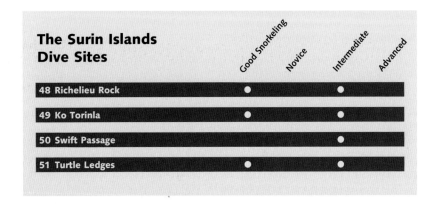

The Surin Islands Dive Sites

	Good Snorkeling	Novice	Intermediate	Advanced
48 Richelieu Rock	●		●	
49 Ko Torinla	●		●	
50 Swift Passage			●	
51 Turtle Ledges	●		●	

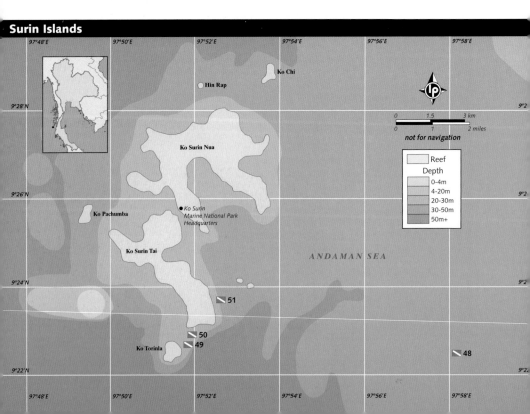

Surin Islands

eastern shorelines are primarily hard coral, closely resembling the Similans' east-side sites. Coral growth here is considered the most developed in all of Thailand, and since some of the most scenic parts are less than 5m deep, it ranks among the country's best snorkeling locales. In fact, Surin is home to Thailand's first underwater nature trail, located in Ao Suthep (Suthep Bay), off the south tip of Ko Surin Tai. About 100m long, the trail is designed for both divers and snorkelers and is marked with eight large, plastic numbered buoys suspended in the water column. Each buoy corresponds to a distinct biological zone and matches a numbered description of a specific reef organism. These "feature creatures" are each depicted on waterproof plastic brochures, available at park headquarters on Ko Surin Nua.

48 Richelieu Rock

While a number of Surin's sites provide good diving opportunities, one place is without question the best of the bunch—a small limestone outcropping known as Richelieu Rock. This site consists of one large pinnacle and several smaller ones that all rise steeply from the sand bottom at about 33m. As the rock barely breaks the surface at low tide, it is easy to see why boats approach this place with caution; it is a notorious navigational hazard. While most captains would just as soon give Richelieu a wide berth, no diver who has been here before would pass up a chance to again explore its life-filled depths.

Although visibility is often limited, experienced divers highly regard this unique spot—the abundance and variety of marine life is truly astounding. Dense colonies of sea anemones sporting shades of green, beige and brilliant purple cover many of the shallower rock surfaces and provide homes for porcelain crabs, shrimp and five different varieties of clownfish. Soft corals adorn

Location: 17km (9 nautical miles) east of Ko Surin Tai

Depth Range: 0-36m (0-118ft)

Access: Live-aboard

Expertise Rating: Intermediate

many of the deeper areas, although the large trees that used to sprout from the sand bottom have sadly vanished in recent years, apparently due to fishing lines and traps being dragged across the bottom.

MARK STRICKLAND

The popular Richelieu Rock attracts many dive boats.

Other invertebrate life includes a wide range of shellfish, as well as a multitude of shrimp, crabs, sea stars, colorful jewel-box urchins and many varieties of nudibranchs. Cephalopods are also common, including both octopuses and cuttlefish, the latter often seen mating and laying eggs along the rocky ledges. During mating, cuttlefish frequently form a ménage à trois, with two males vying over the attention of one female. Though all cuttlefish can change color, mating males often put on a technicolor display, with ripples of electric purple, gold, black and chartreuse flowing over the length of their bodies.

Richelieu Rock is also one of the few places where you may see a rare shovel-nose ray. Also known as giant guitarfish, these bizarre animals have the flattened head and ventrally located mouth of a stingray combined with the body and tail of a shark. These wary creatures can grow to more than 3m long. More common and certainly more approachable are large marbled stingrays, typically seen around the deeper edges of the reef, resting on the bottom or hovering in the current over soft corals. Spotted eagle rays, the ever-graceful cousins of the marbled ray, are also occasional visitors to Richelieu.

Nearly every imaginable variety of bony fish is found here as well, including many species of butterflyfish, wrasse, damselfish, lionfish and a host of other reef dwellers. Among the most abundant species are scorpionfish, which are amazingly adept at blending in with their surroundings. Be especially careful where you put your hands, because many things that look like rocks are not!

A number of eel species live here as well, including giant, whitemouth, fimbriated, snowflake, bar-tail and zebra morays. Schooling fish like fusiliers and snappers are also prevalent, in addition to open-water predators like rainbow runners, mackerel and barracuda. One schooling fish deserves special mention: Look for a huge school of bigeye jacks on the up-current side of the rock, where they often circle divers en masse, creating a living maelstrom of fish.

Another of Richelieu Rock's claims to fame is the impressive incidence of whale shark sightings. Although the number of encounters varies considerably from one year to the next, Richelieu normally ranks among the best places in the world to see these amazing animals, especially from February through May. If you are lucky enough to encounter a whale shark, please remember to look but not touch. Even gentle contact tends to scare them away.

MARK STRICKLAND
While mating, the male cuttlefish displays kaleidoscopic colors.

Whale Sharks: The World's Largest Fish

Growing to more than 12m (40ft) long and weighing in excess of 18,000kg (20 tons), whale sharks are true sharks that grow to whale-like proportions. Fortunately for swimmers and divers, these leviathans are among the most docile of creatures. They spend much of their lives swimming placidly near the surface, feeding on plankton and small fish strained from the water with their specialized gill rakers.

MARK STRICKLAND

Often a diver's first impression of a whale shark is that of a sudden, total eclipse of the sun as the massive beast passes overhead. At this point, even experienced divers are unable to act blasé; it is not every day one is confronted with a fish the size of a boat! Then, as the unmistakable silhouette glides past, adrenaline levels slowly subside, and curiosity and delight quickly replace any initial apprehension. Anyone lucky enough to have encountered one of these enormous animals will tell you that being in the water with such a creature is an incredible experience.

Whale sharks themselves seldom act very excited about much of anything and usually behave indifferently to divers and snorkelers. Sometimes, however, they seem intrigued by bubble-blowing humans, occasionally nuzzling divers or even boats. Although these animals often allow divers to swim close alongside, don't misconstrue this as an invitation to touch them or grab on for a ride. While these practices have been promoted in the past, it is now widely recognized that such interaction generally alarms the animal, causing it to leave the area and end the encounter. In the long run, the rewards of passive interaction will prove far richer.

Occurring worldwide in tropical and temperate waters, whale sharks are considered rare; few divers ever see one. A few places in the world, however, have become known as "hot spots" for whale sharks. Although these gentle giants show up occasionally at many Thai reefs (particularly from February to May), a few special places offer better odds of seeing them. In the Gulf of Thailand, Chumphon Pinnacles offers perhaps the best chance, followed by Ko Losin and Sail Rock. In the Andaman Sea, Richelieu Rock, Hin Muang and Hin Daeng are the clear favorites.

Naturally, the incidence of whale shark sightings varies from year to year. Unfortunately, however, sightings have drastically declined over the last few seasons. It is not clear why, as very little is known about whale shark populations and their migratory patterns. Some very discouraging activities may have had an impact: According to the U.S.-based Shark Research Institute, dedicated whale shark fisheries have been established in Taiwan, the Philippines, Indonesia, India and Malaysia. Thankfully, no such fishery exists in Thailand, but with a migratory species like whale sharks, the actions of neighboring countries can have a profound effect locally.

49 Ko Torinla

A small island lying about 1km south-west of Ko Surin Tai, Ko Torinla offers several potentially good dive sites. Perhaps the best of these is on the northeast side, where a sloping hard-coral reef runs parallel to shore. Several moorings are located offshore of a small sandy beach in 10 to 15m, making an ideal place to begin your dive. From there, you can swim parallel to the reef either north or south of the moorings.

In most areas the reef bottoms out at 15 to 18m, where the sandy seafloor is home to blue-spotted stingrays, along

Location: Northeast side of Ko Torinla

Depth Range: 0-18m (0-60ft)

Access: Live-aboard

Expertise Rating: Intermediate

with occasional Jenkins and marbled rays. Divers frequently see leopard and white-tip reef sharks here.

Moving up the reef slope, you'll find an excellent variety of hard corals, along with some nice fans and whip corals. Fish life is also abundant, with a wide spectrum of colorful reef species. Schooling fish like fusiliers and batfish gather here, as do huge bumphead parrotfish, a species seldom seen elsewhere in the region. Hawksbill turtles are encountered quite regularly. The shallower areas feature lots of healthy coral and fish life, making this an ideal multilevel dive, as well as a great snorkeling site.

MARK STRICKLAND
A typical Ko Torinla reef scene.

50 Swift Passage

One especially exciting Surin-area dive is Swift Passage, the narrow pass that separates Ko Surin Tai and Ko Torinla (the smaller island just to the south). The passage is aptly named; strong currents are very common here. When conducted as a drift dive, however, this is actually a bonus—you can cruise effortlessly over the reef without having to kick a stroke.

Watch the constant parade of marine life for schooling batfish, jacks and mackerel. Blacktip and whitetip reef sharks are also seen here with fair frequency, as are

Location: South end of Ko Surin Tai

Depth Range: 12-27m (40-90ft)

Access: Live-aboard

Expertise Rating: Intermediate

bumphead parrotfish, typically residing amid the shallow hard-coral formations. Hawksbill turtles are especially abundant in this area, with up to 10 individuals reported on a single dive.

Sea Gypsies

Among Surin's many interesting features is a small Chao Lay village on Ko Surin Tai. Culturally and ethnically separate from the Thais, the Chao Lay exist in only a few isolated areas along the Thai and Myanmar Andaman Coast. These seafaring people—often referred to as sea gypsies—live a spartan existence, shunning most of the trappings of modern society in favor of time-honored traditions. A shy and reserved people, most depend on the sea for their livelihood. Although fishing has always been their main priority, selling seashells to tourists is increasingly common.

If logistics allow (a fairly high tide is needed to bring a dinghy ashore here), a visit to these villages offers a glimpse into a unique culture. As you wander amid the huts and boats, remember that you are a guest in someone else's home and be respectful of your hosts' right to privacy. The villages may be closed to visitors during the full moon in March, when the Chao Lay hold ceremonies involving ancestor worship. To check availability before planning a visit, call the Ko Surin Marine National Park office at ☎ (76) 491 378.

51 Turtle Ledges

Among the best of Surin's east-side sites is Turtle Ledges, a long sloping reef that

Location: East side of Ko Surin Tai

Depth Range: 0-24m (0-79ft)

Access: Live-aboard

Expertise Rating: Intermediate

An elegant but awkward juvenile pinnate batfish.

MARK STRICKLAND

borders the east side of Ko Surin Tai. The wide range of fish life includes seldom-seen species like yellowmask angelfish, barramundi cod, Andaman foxface and the peculiar yet beautiful juvenile pinnate batfish. With their striking black and orange coloration and unusual vertical body orientation, these youngsters are truly a sight to behold. As the site's name implies, this is also a favorite haunt of hawksbill turtles, often seen resting amid the coral or cruising over the reef's edge.

Gentle conditions prevail here, with minimal currents making for easy diving. On the rare occasion that currents do pick up, they generally run parallel to the reef, allowing effortless drift diving.

Myanmar Dive Sites

The country of Myanmar is home to a vast number of islands, coral reefs and banks, all of which lie to the north and west of Thailand. Because of the distance to Myanmar's most popular dive areas—the Mergui Archipelago and the Burma Banks—dive excursions are limited to live-aboards based out of Phuket, Thailand, and Kawthaung, Myanmar. Known to Thais as Ko Song (meaning "Second Island"), Kawthaung is also referred to by its colonial name of Victoria Point. This small fishing town is the gateway to the region's dive sites—even live-aboards from Phuket need to stop here to go through customs. While Thailand-based vessels usually dive in the Similans and Surin areas as well as Myanmar, boats based in Kawthaung generally specialize in their national waters. Typical itineraries range from 4 to 10 days, regardless of where the boats are based. If you are shopping for a dive trip to Myanmar, keep in mind that nearly all dive operators still refer to the country by its former name, Burma.

EDWARD SNIJDERS

While diving here is similar in some ways to diving in Thailand, there are also many differences, including an abundance of uncommon and unusual marine life. Another positive point is the relative scarcity of dive boats here compared with Thai waters, at least for the time being.

Mergui Archipelago & Burma Banks Dive Sites	Good Snorkeling	Novice	Intermediate	Advanced
52 Western Rocky Island			●	
53 Fan Forest Pinnacle			●	
54 High Rock			●	
55 North Twin Island			●	
56 North Twin Plateau			●	
57 Three Islets (In Through the Out Door)	●		●	
58 Black Rock				●
59 Northeast Little Torres Island	●		●	
60 Burma Banks				●

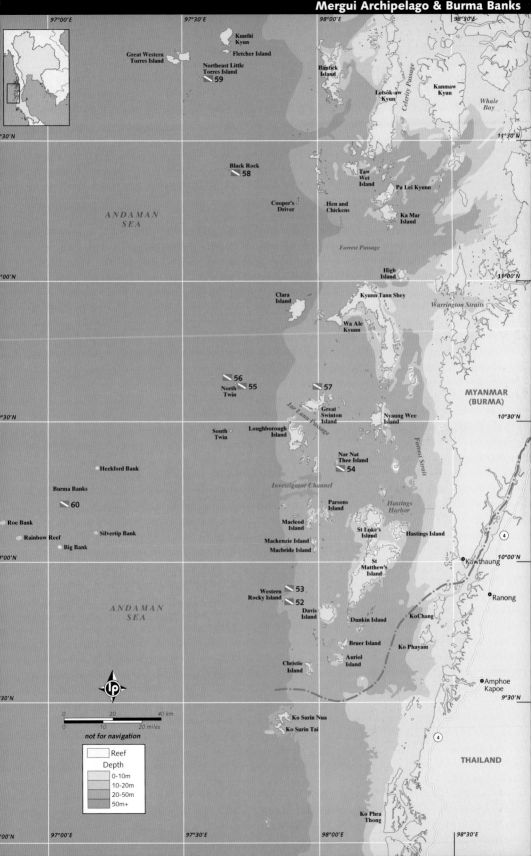

97°00'E

97°30'E

98°00'E

98°30'E

Kunthi
Kyun

Fletcher Island

Great Western
Torres Island

Northeast Little
Torres Island
59

Bamick
Island

Letsôk-aw
Kyun

Kanmaw
Kyun

*Whale
Bay*

Celerity Passage

11°30'N

Black Rock
58

Taw
Wet
Island

Pa Lei Kyunn

Cooper's
Driver

Hen and
Chickens

Ka Mar
Island

*A N D A M A N
S E A*

Forrest Passage

High
Island

11°00'N

Clara
Island

Kyunn Tann Shey

Warrington Straits

Wa Ale
Kyunn

56

55

North
Twin

57

Iar Lann Passage

MYANMAR
(BURMA)

10°30'N

Great
Swinton
Island

Nyaung Wee
Island

South
Twin

Loughborough
Island

Forrest Strait

Nar Nat
Thee Island
54

Heckford Bank

Investigator Channel

Burma Banks
60

Parsons
Island

*Hastings
Harbor*

Roe Bank

Macleod
Island

St Luke's
Island

Hastings Island

Rainbow Reef

Silvertip Bank

Mackenzie Island

Big Bank

Macbride Island

④

Kawthaung

10°00'N

St
Matthew's
Island

Western
Rocky Island
53

52

Ranong

Davis
Island

Dunkin Island

KoChang

*A N D A M A N
S E A*

Bruer Island

Ko Phayam

Christie
Island

Auriol
Island

Amphoe
Kapoe

9°30'N

Ⓤ

0   20   40 km

0   10   20 miles

not for navigation

④

Ko Surin Nua

Ko Surin Tai

THAILAND

Reef

Depth

0-10m

10-20m

20-50m

50m+

Ko Phra
Thong

97°00'E

97°30'E

98°00'E

98°30'E

Entry Procedures

Visitors to the Mergui Archipelago and the Burma Banks must clear Myanmar customs and immigration, normally at Kawthaung. Entry formalities are surprisingly straightforward, with few delays or difficulties. Though the border was temporarily closed in 1999 due to conflicts between the two countries, it seems likely that entry into Myanmar will continue without problems. Dive operators usually take care of entry details, so you need not be too concerned with the actual procedure. Nonetheless, it is probably a good idea to check on border status before booking a trip.

Valid passports are required, along with an entry fee, currently set at US$100 to $130 depending on your destination and duration of stay. Although entering Myanmar via Kawthaung is completely proper as far as local authorities are concerned, it is still only a "semiofficial" entry into the country. For this reason, passports are not stamped, nor does such entry allow you to travel elsewhere in Myanmar. Under the present system, you are strictly limited to the Mergui Archipelago and the Burma Banks, according to the specific itinerary of the trip you have joined.

Normally there is no need for separate currency, as both U.S. dollars and Thai baht are widely accepted in Kawthaung. Typically, divers spend less than a day here while awaiting departure on a live-aboard vessel, and provided this is the case, it is not necessary to change money. However, should you wish to stay longer, you may be required to purchase $300 worth of foreign exchange certificates.

Mergui Archipelago

Just north of the Surin Islands, an imaginary line divides Thai waters from Myanmar's Mergui Archipelago. Also known as the Myeik Archipelago, this immense area covers approximately 36,000 sq km (14,000 sq miles) and includes roughly 800 islands. Diving here is still in its infancy, as the entire region has been off-limits to outsiders since the late 1940s. After several years of negotiation by Phuket dive operators, the archipelago was opened for tourism in 1997, yet much of the area remains unexplored.

The islands are similar to their Thai counterparts, with rugged, high-profile limestone and granite topography. One obvious difference, aside from the sheer number of Myanmar islands, is their unspoiled terrestrial scenery. Dense brush and rainforest cover most areas above the high-tide line, while vast stretches of mangroves and magnificent white-sand beaches are interspersed with rocky headlands, tidal creeks and a few freshwater rivers. Though several of the larger islands are home to small communities of Moken "sea gypsies," the vast majority are uninhabited and largely untouched by humans.

Underwater, this region offers scenic reefs, fascinating topography and prolific fish and invertebrate life. One of the main attractions for divers is the strong possibility of seeing big animals, especially sharks and rays. More dependable, however, is the tremendous variety of smaller fish and reef creatures, including many unusual species, some of which are rarely encountered in Thai waters. Add to this the allure of diving where few people have before and you've got all the ingredients for a top-notch dive destination. Considering the vast number of islands and reefs, many more dive sites are undoubtedly waiting to be discovered.

The diving here has tremendous potential, yet serious environmental problems threaten the reefs. Trawling and longline fishing have put heavy pressure on fish populations and the marine habitat in general, but the biggest threat is blast fishing with dynamite, which Myanmar has done little to discourage. You are likely to hear bombs go off at least once during a multi-day trip anywhere in the archipelago. Virtually all Mergui sites show at least some evidence of blast fishing, from craters of broken coral to piles of orange cup corals and even huge chunks of rock that have been blasted off vertical walls.

Despite the environmental threats, the diving in the Mergui is still excellent. Even at sites that are bombed regularly, soft corals, anemones and gorgonian fans usually survive undamaged, as do nudibranchs, cuttlefish, octopuses and other invertebrates. Fish that lack swim bladders (like sharks, rays and moray eels) also seem unaffected, unless the explosion is very close. Also, since many fish move from reef to reef, new fish seem to show up all the time.

In addition to dedicated dive trips, several companies offer eco-adventure trips in the Mergui Archipelago, combining sailing, snorkeling, diving, beach-combing, island exploration and, in some cases, kayaking. It is too early to say what this area's long-term prospects are, but hopefully, increasing interest in ecotourism will provide enough incentive for the authorities to take action and protect the reefs before it is too late.

MARK STRICKLAND

A Moken "sea gypsy" cleans a fishing boat.

52 Western Rocky Island

Myanmar authorities have declared Western Rocky Island off-limits to dive boats for "security reasons" since late 1998 and have not indicated when this restriction may be lifted. When accessible, Western Rocky, a small limestone island with several nearby outcroppings, offers fascinating underwater topography, big-animal potential and a plethora of invertebrate and fish life. The main island can be circumnavigated on a single tank, although it would take many dives to see everything this site has to offer.

After investigating the perimeter, swim east-northeast from the island's eastern tip. You'll cross a narrow sand channel before reaching the first of two groups of pinnacles. The nearest group consists of

Location: 78km (42 nautical miles) west-southwest of Kawthaung

Depth Range: 3-40m (10-130ft)

Access: Live-aboard

Expertise Rating: Intermediate

four spires connected by a common base at 24m; the more distant group is a pair of somewhat larger rocks with a similar structure. Both groups reach well above the surface. East-northeast beyond the base of the more distant pinnacles is a huge field of orange fan corals, starting at about 30m deep and continuing beyond recreational diving limits. The nearly vertical sides of the pinnacles and the main island are ideal for multilevel dives.

Like most limestone formations, these structures are honeycombed with crevices that provide superb cover for shy reef creatures. A large tunnel runs completely through the island, and there are several smaller caverns and a huge archway. The most obvious entrance to the tunnel is at 21m on the island's south side, where a large A-shaped opening leads to a roomy inner chamber. Here a shell-and-rubble bottom slopes uphill slightly before dropping down to 24m, where the chamber narrows to a fairly small exit on the north side of the island.

Several species of crab and shrimp, murex and cowrie shells, bigeye snappers and robust fusiliers and even spiny lobsters live within the tunnel. The lobsters are crucial prey for the large tawny

MARK STRICKLAND
Bigeye snappers hover over soft coral.

nurse sharks that sometimes inhabit the tunnel. If you are lucky, you may get a look at these amiable creatures, some of which measure nearly 3.5m long.

While at least a glimmer of daylight is usually visible from any point inside the tunnel, this is an advanced cavern dive because of its depth and distance between openings. Be sure to keep your fins off the bottom to avoid kicking up silt—even the easiest cavern dive can become a nightmare if visibility is reduced. To further ensure safety and enjoyment, no more than six divers should be inside at a time.

Regardless of whether or not you enter the tunnel, this site has a wealth of marine life, with something to see at every depth. In deeper areas, stingrays,

whitetip reef and leopard sharks lie on the sand bottom, while grey reef and spinner sharks sometimes patrol in the distance. You'll see plenty of reef fish as well, including blue-ringed angelfish, red emperor snapper, red-bar anthias and many varieties of moray eels.

Invertebrates are also well represented, with a wide assortment of nudibranchs, shellfish, feather stars, anemones and hermit crabs. On occasion, even rarities like clawed reef lobsters, harlequin shrimp and frogfish are encountered. While only limited hard coral remains after years of blast fishing, large portions of the vertical walls are covered with orange cup corals and small, multihued soft corals. It is still an extremely scenic site.

53 Fan Forest Pinnacle

Fan Forest Pinnacle, like Western Rocky, has been off-limits to dive boats for "security reasons" since late 1998. The authorities have not indicated when this restriction may be lifted. Just 10km north of Western Rocky, this large limestone pinnacle rises from more than 45m deep to within 5m of the surface. Accordingly, it offers a good multilevel profile, although the shallowest portions are rather barren.

Perhaps the site's most striking feature is a tremendous number of huge, undamaged orange fan corals, most of which are below 30m. Blue-ringed angelfish, lionfish and coral trout are among the most common reef fish, in addition to midwater species like jacks, barracuda and batfish. You'll also have a good possibility of encountering big animals like leopard, grey reef and whitetip reef sharks, mantas and eagle rays.

Location: 10km (5.4 nautical miles) north of Western Rocky Island

Depth Range: 5-40m+ (16-130ft+)

Access: Live-aboard

Expertise Rating: Intermediate

MARK STRICKLAND

A lionfish hides amid orange fan corals.

54 High Rock

High Rock is easily recognized from a distance, as it consists of a small island with a single tree on top. Below the surface on the north and east sides, limestone walls drop almost vertically, bottoming out at 18 to 24m. On the south and west sides, the terrain drops more gradually to the sandy seafloor. In spite of frequent blast fishing, marine life thrives here, with dense growths of orange cup coral covering many of the deeper rocks and vertical walls. Below 21m, huge green tubastrea coral and large black-coral bushes dominate the seascape, complemented by red harp gorgonians, pastel-green rope sponges and feather stars of most every color. Small soft corals are prevalent in moderate depths on the south side, while you'll find several huge soft-coral trees at 24m on the north end.

Location: 70km (38 nautical miles) northwest of Kawthaung

Depth Range: 0-30m (0-98ft)

Access: Live-aboard

Expertise Rating: Intermediate

Although the scenery is beautiful, this site description would not be complete without mentioning the old fishing nets and lines that lie tangled amid the coral in some areas. While this jumble of gear does nothing to improve the aesthetics or health of the reef, it at least provides ideal holdfasts for the many tigertail seahorses that live here; apparently, these old nets are their favorite habitat.

Other resident fish life includes small reef species like flatheads (normally found half-buried in the sand) and giant blennies (which are usually seen at safety-stop depth). High Rock also offers a chance to encounter camouflage experts like harlequin ghost pipefish and frogfish. Other frequently seen creatures include venomous urchins, banded sea snakes and entire armies of hingebeak shrimp.

MARK STRICKLAND

Sunset accentuates High Rock's unique form.

55 North Twin Island

Although this island has several diveable areas, the best site is **Western Ridge**. A shallow rock pinnacle lies about 5m below the surface several hundred meters west of the island's south tip. From there, a long rocky ridge slopes gradually to the west, eventually reaching 36m or more.

Diving is best on the north side of the ridge, where typical scenery consists of

Location: 124km (67 nautical miles) northwest of Kawthaung

Depth Range: 5-36m (16-118ft)

Access: Live-aboard

Expertise Rating: Intermediate

large sea fans, small but colorful soft corals and a variety of hard corals, all attached to the rocky substrate. Though the south side appears rather barren compared with the north, fish life often includes schooling fish such as queenfish and rainbow runners, as well as reef species like jeweled and giant moray eels, blue-ringed angelfish, goatfish and many others. Around the deeper edges there is a chance of bigger animals, with occasional sightings of whitetip reef sharks, grey reef sharks and tawny nurse sharks. Even bull sharks have been seen here.

MARK STRICKLAND

Sea anemones frequently host eggshell shrimp.

56　North Twin Plateau

This expansive site consists of dozens of large, widely scattered granite boulders resting on a rocky plateau at 24 to 30m. This plateau is in turn surrounded by a gradually sloping sandy bottom, resulting in topography reminiscent of the western Similan Islands. Marine life is healthy and abundant, yet tends to be scattered over a fairly large area. Therefore, a good strategy is to start at the deeper edges and work inward, making an effort to cover some distance rather than linger at any one place. You'll have a better chance of encountering the leopard and whitetip reef sharks that inhabit the reef's outer perimeter, while taking in more scenery.

Many of the deeper areas are populated with dense forests of orange fan corals, and soft corals sprout from rocky

Location: 1.9km (1 nautical mile) northwest of North Twin Island

Depth Range: 15-40m+ (50-130ft+)

Access: Live-aboard

Expertise Rating: Intermediate

crevices at moderate depths. Surrounded as it is by open water, this site attracts a wide range of mid-water predators, including rainbow runners, bonitos, queenfish and lots of pickhandle and great barracuda. Sandbar sharks—easily distinguished from other species by their tall dorsal fins—have reportedly been seen here.

57 Three Islets (In Through the Out Door)

Location: 99km (53 nautical miles) northwest of Kawthaung

Depth Range: 0-27m (0-89ft)

Access: Live-aboard

Expertise Rating: Intermediate

This large area consists of one small island and two large rocks, all of which rise well above the surface. Each could be considered a separate site; there is no way to see them all on a single dive, or even a full day of diving. All three islets are perfectly suited for multilevel profiles, with thriving marine life from the bottom to the surface. While the main island probably offers the best diving, both smaller islets are also worth exploring. The south islet features a submerged reef that nearly connects with the main island. Assuming you use currents to your advantage, it is normally an easy swim between the two. The north islet, on the other hand, is at least 100m from the main island and is best done as a separate dive.

Underwater, the combination of unusual topography and a tremendous variety of creatures makes this one of the best dive sites in the Mergui Archipelago. Nearly every square meter is riddled with crevices that provide shelter and holdfasts for an enormous volume of fish and invertebrate life. Typically, from the moment you leave the surface, you'll be surrounded by schools of silversides and fusiliers that frantically dash about trying to avoid the ravenous jacks and bonitos that harass them around the clock.

Before you look at the reef, it is worth doing a quick survey of the surrounding sandy seafloor. Although it may appear barren at first glance, a closer look will reveal a wealth of interesting creatures, including tube anemones, burrowing sea cucumbers and several unusually beautiful varieties of sea stars. While you are over the sand, look at the large brown sea anemones, as they frequently host eggshell shrimp, as well as sebae clownfish, a species seldom seen at other sites.

MARK STRICKLAND

Fimbriated, white-eyed and jeweled morays share a hole.

Moving over to the reef base, you will find sheer walls and dense colonies of orange cup corals around much of the perimeter. Elsewhere, the substrate steps down more gradually, creating an ideal base for rope sponges, whip corals and huge stands of green tubastrea coral. Feather stars are especially prolific and often provide homes for various shrimp, squat lobsters and crinoid clingfish. These reefs are also blessed with some very impressive red and yellow gorgonian fans, some of which grow in only 3m of water. Have a good look at these, since well-camouflaged spindle cowries often hide amid the branches, along with hawkfish and occasional gorgonian crabs. Other noteworthy creatures found here include basket stars, jewel-box urchins, cuttlefish, squid and several species of cowries.

Fish life is also extremely diverse, with marbled rays, false and true stonefish, flatheads, Schultz's pipefish, badger cling-fish, tigertail seahorses and several species of morays, in addition to most of the usual players. This is also one of the better places to see creatures like harlequin shrimp and harlequin ghost pipefish.

Aside from marine life, one of the most outstanding features of this area is a large canyon on the north end of the main island. While the rock walls making up the outer portions of this area are rather barren, there is a fair chance of encountering up to 12 or so semi-resident grey reef sharks. Generally inhabiting open coral reefs, these sharks are not usually known to hang around enclosed areas; it's a very unusual environment for this species. Typically these animals are not aggressive toward divers, but be careful not to corner them in the canyon; grey reef sharks have been known to vigorously defend their territory in such circumstances. The best approach here is to keep close to the rock wall on your right, and slow down as you enter the narrow parts of the canyon.

When you come to a rock archway, stop and have a good look around. If you are lucky, you may get to see several grey reefs patrolling this somewhat confined area, milling around in mid-water. If the sharks are present, just stay put on the bottom and enjoy watching them until they leave the area, which is usually within a minute or two. Once they leave, or if they are not around, continue into the canyon until you pass under the archway, then follow the wall to the right. Here you will see a tall, fairly wide opening to a tunnel that runs completely through the island and exits on the east side at about 15m. Plenty of natural light is available, but you may wish to bring a dive light to fully enjoy the colorful cup corals and yellow sponges that

Tawny nurse sharks may be found resting on the deep bottom.

line the tunnel walls. Fish are plentiful here as well, with schools of small yellow snappers and copper sweepers hovering throughout the cavern.

Just below the main tunnel you will find a smaller cavern that runs roughly parallel to the main passage, with only enough room for two or three divers at a time. The site's second name, In Through the Out Door, is a clever ref-erence to these twin tunnel entrances. Although this cavern also has an en-trance at either end and is not especially dangerous, it can be very tricky if a big swell is running—be sure to check with your dive leader before entering. Be sure not to disturb the several huge (more than 3m long) tawny nurse sharks that sometimes rest within the crevices.

58 Black Rock

Black Rock is a natural magnet for marine life. The small, steep limestone island's underwater terrain consists of sloping reef on the north and east sides, while the south and west sides are mostly walls, dropping vertically from the sur-face to around 27m. From there the slope is more gradual, stepping down to 45m or more.

Though you'll find good diving all around the island, some of the best scenery is off the southwest corner, where, at 24 to 39m, an incredibly dense mosaic of small soft corals, orange cup coral and

Location: 190km (103 nautical miles) north-northwest of Kawthaung

Depth Range: 3-40m+ (10-130ft+)

Access: Live-aboard

Expertise Rating: Advanced

feather stars covers the large rocks. Of particular interest are colonies of small tiger-striped anemones that cling to fan coral and gorgonian skeletons; these

A golden wentletrap snail feeds on an orange cup coral, then deposits eggs in the empty skeleton.

anemones are seldom seen outside of the Mergui Archipelago. Also check out the gravel bottom at about 30m for small but brilliantly colored filament wrasse, usually seen zipping around, flexing their fins and generally showing off.

Other reef fish are also abundant, especially black-spotted pufferfish, spotted hawkfish, scorpionfish and blue-ringed angelfish. Deeper areas also see frequent visits by schooling fish like pinjalo snappers and jacks, while fusiliers are common at every depth. Sharks are a real possibility as well, with a chance of seeing leopard, grey reef, spinner and even bull sharks; spotted eagle rays and mantas also make fairly regular appearances.

On the island's north side, whitetip reef sharks regularly patrol the deeper slopes, along with schools of rainbow runners, blue-lined barracuda, and tall-fin batfish. Some especially large giant morays, as well as jeweled, zebra, fimbriated and white-eyed morays, are some of the regularly seen moray species—you may even see the latter two sharing the same crevice.

Other frequently seen creatures include octopuses and cuttlefish, both of which may be seen at nearly any depth, and *Saron* shrimp, normally found in shallow rubble areas when they emerge from their lairs at dusk. On the vertical walls, look for golden wentletrap snails. These tiny yellow gastropods extend a strawlike proboscis to devour their favorite prey, orange cup corals. Once the coral is consumed, female snails fill the empty skeleton with clusters of sticky yellow eggs that perfectly imitate the coral's stinging tentacles.

Safety stops are rarely boring at Black Rock, as some of the most fascinating critters live in the surge zone. Of particular interest are the many varieties of cowries, nudibranchs, shrimp and unusual hermit crab species. The shallow portions of the east end are especially attractive in the early morning, late afternoon and on cloudy days, when the dozens of magnificent sea anemones retract their tentacles, revealing their vivid pink and purple bases.

While Black Rock is often an easy dive, strong currents are not unusual. If you are diving the west end when the current

MARK STRICKLAND

Crinoids adorn this large sea fan.

is flowing west, take care not to end up past the deep westernmost rocks. Down-currents can also be very strong at these times, making it difficult to get back to shallow reef areas. That said, you have no reason to be leery about diving here; just be sure to ask your dive leader about conditions before jumping in.

59 Northeast Little Torres Island

A small island surrounded by deep open water, this site has a good selection of reef fish and invertebrates, along with a reasonable chance of seeing sharks and other big animals.

Location: 228km (123 nautical miles) north-northwest of Kawthaung

Depth Range: 10-40m+ (30-130ft+)

Access: Live-aboard

Expertise Rating: Intermediate

Perhaps the best area to start your dive is at the western tip of the narrow rock ridge that breaks the surface in several places off the island's west end. As you descend, drift with the current and follow the steeply sloping rock face to around 30m, where the seascape is dominated by large fan corals. Keep an eye toward the open water in this area, as spinner, bull and grey reef sharks sometimes patrol just off the reef. It's also good to watch your depth here, as it is easy to go deeper than planned.

As you drift past the point, work your way around the corner to the east and follow the reef. Depending on the current's direction, you will end up on either the north or south side of the ridge. Both areas are similar, with gently sloping terrain and a scattering of hard corals, anemones and sea whips.

Most typical reef fish are present, including blue-ringed angelfish, various triggerfish, wrasses and others, along with schooling fish like fusiliers and snappers. On occasion, squadrons of mobula rays (a small species of manta) pass by in midwater. It's worth looking toward the surface now and then.

EDWARD SNIDERS

A diver is surrounded by silversides at Little Torres.

Burma Banks

Far offshore of the Mergui Archipelago lies a series of submerged mountaintops collectively known as the Burma Banks. Surrounded by open sea in all directions, these remote, widely separated reefs were not accurately plotted on nautical charts until they were extensively dived in the early 1990s. After a series of exploratory trips by several Phuket-based live-aboards, five banks were located. Other boats followed almost immediately, and the Burma Banks quickly became a popular dive destination.

The main reason people go to the Banks is to see sharks. Altogether, at least nine species have been seen here, including rare encounters with tiger sharks and scalloped hammerheads. Others like grey reef and leopard sharks are not exactly rare, but sightings are infrequent. Reef whitetip sharks are probably the most common species at the Banks, yet they tend to be very shy, so most divers see them only from a distance. Perhaps the most approachable species are tawny nurse sharks, typically found resting under coral heads or patrolling lazily over the reeftop. Curious and unafraid, they often swim right up to divers, providing excellent photo opportunities. The real stars at the Banks, however, are silvertip sharks—a species seldom seen elsewhere. Solid, powerfully built, yet supremely graceful, they move with the easy confidence that comes with being at the top of the food chain. Readily identified by the white edges on all their fins, these animals leave a lasting impression and are ample reason for visiting the Banks.

Diving at the Banks is nearly always exciting and rewarding, but it is not for everyone. This is open-ocean diving—no sheltered anchorages or islands to hide behind, just open sea in all directions. Most sites are quite deep, and strong, changeable currents are very common. All this should not imply that the Banks are not worth the effort. For experienced divers looking for an unusual environment, high-voltage excitement and big-animal encounters, the Burma Banks are definitely the place to be.

MARK STRICKLAND

Painted crayfish extend their long antennae from a colorful Burma Banks crevice.

Deep Diving

Opportunities to dive deep abound in Thailand. Many attractions are beyond 40m (130ft), the recognized maximum depth limit of sport diving. Before venturing beyond these limits, it is imperative that divers be specially trained in deep diving and/or technical diving.

Classes will teach you to recognize symptoms of nitrogen narcosis and perform proper decompression procedures when doing deep or repetitive deep dives. Remember, emergency facilities in Thailand are limited. Know your limits and don't push your luck when it comes to depth.

60 Burma Banks

The majority of diveable areas at the Banks are fairly level, broad plateaus, typically about 1km in diameter. Minimum depths are 21 to 24m at most of them, making for rather short bottom times. The water surrounding all of the Banks is quite deep, averaging 250 to 300m; there are no walls within recreational diving depths.

Location: 170km (92 nautical miles) west-northwest of Kawthaung

Depth Range: 15-40m+ (49-130ft+)

Access: Live-aboard

Expertise Rating: Advanced

Marine life is healthy and abundant in most areas, although the diversity of species does not compare with many inshore sites. Because of their proximity to deep water, the Banks are an excellent place to see open-water predators like rainbow runners, bonitos and husky dogtooth tuna. Occasionally, big animals like eagle rays and mantas also show up, usually cruising along the reef's deeper edges. Most of the Banks have some live coral, but you'll also see areas of dead coral and rubble, probably caused by crown-of-thorns sea star invasions. Even these areas have interesting features, as some of the many huge, ancient coral bommies are bizarrely shaped. Although hard corals are the norm, excellent soft corals grow in certain places, especially deeper portions of **Silvertip Bank.**

Silvertip Bank is one of the closest banks to Kawthaung and is also the shal-

lowest, making it by far the most popular. As at the other Banks, most of the diveable area here is an expansive, coral-covered plateau. Unlike the others, however, it is as shallow as 15m in some places, allowing for a longer dive.

Silvertip's sloping drop-offs are another feature not seen at the other Banks. Two areas, one on the eastern edge of the plateau and the other on the western edge, feature steeply sloping terrain that drops from about 18m to beyond 40m. These areas tend to attract more marine life than other portions of the reef, so it is definitely worth having a look around here.

Both drop-offs make good choices for morning dives, since the best marine life tends to be fairly deep. Start your dive by descending to at least 36m, where you'll find the nicest soft corals and gorgonians, as well as large barrel sponges, especially on the west side. Impressive colonies of cabbage coral intermingle with fields of staghorn and occasional boulder corals on these deeper slopes. The east drop-off usually has more fish action than the west, with large schools of pyramid butterflyfish, fusiliers and redtooth triggerfish hovering above many areas. As you work your way up the slope, soft corals become less common, with a higher prevalence of hard corals. Save some time to explore the plateau, where you'll see plenty of interesting coral formations and a variety of fish.

It is a good idea to keep an eye on the open water, since predators like rainbow runners, dogtooth tuna and jacks make regular patrols along the drop-offs. Sharks (particularly reef whitetips) are often seen resting on the sandy bottom. Silvertip sharks also make an appearance on nearly every dive, mostly around the deeper slopes, but also on the reeftop. Reaching lengths of nearly 2.5m, these sleek predators command instant respect, yet pose little threat to sightseeing divers.

Currents can be very strong here, especially along the drop-offs. However, they frequently run parallel to the slope, creating ideal conditions for an effortless drift dive. Down-currents occur from time to time, yet seldom last more than a few minutes; normally it is best just to stay put and wait it out by digging your hands into the sand or ducking behind a coral head.

As the name suggests, **Big Bank** is significantly larger than the others are, measuring nearly 2km in diameter. While much of the reef offers decent diving, two areas are particularly interesting. One of these is along the western edge of the bank, which gently slopes from about 24 to 39m. While certainly not a spectacular drop-off, you'll find a somewhat higher density of fish and corals here than at other parts of this bank. The western edge is also the only place in the Andaman Sea where the rare Strickland's triggerfish has been reported; previously this species was thought to be only in the Mascarenes (an island group off the coast of Madagascar, in the

MARK STRICKLAND

Diver swims over large double table coral at Rainbow Reef.

Indian Ocean). Big Bank's other noteworthy area is several hundred meters east of the western edge, where you'll find an especially high concentration of huge, strangely shaped coral bommies. Several tawny nurse sharks also seem to favor this habitat; they are sometimes seen swimming single file, nose to tail across the reef.

Similar in many ways to the other Banks, **Rainbow Reef** is another large, coral-covered plateau. The one feature that sets it apart is an unusual predominance of table corals, actually a flattened version of *Acropora* staghorn. Some of these colonies have grown to tremendous proportions, reaching 5m or more in diameter. Unfortunately, an outbreak of crown-of-thorns sea stars consumed many of these corals in the mid-1990s, but there are still plenty of live colonies.

Roe Bank is the most distant bank from Kawthaung and is also fairly deep, so it is not frequently dived these days. Like most of the Banks, the plateau is fairly large, roughly 1km in diameter. Much of this area is quite barren, but somewhere near the center is an extensive area of healthy reef, with fields of staghorn coral stretching beyond the limit of visibility. Nearby, massive fossil coral bommies dot the seascape. One looks very much like an old castle, complete with ramparts and windows. Reef fish include schools of surgeonfish, batfish and fusiliers, along with occasional guineafowl pufferfish. As at most of the Banks, you've got a good chance of seeing mid-water predators like rainbow runners, bonito and dogtooth tuna. Reef whitetip, tawny nurse and silvertip sharks also reside in the area.

Located well northeast of the other Banks, **Heckford** is quite deep; most areas are at or below 24m. Its location and depth, along with the absence of large coral formations, probably account for the lack of interest in this site; it is seldom dived. Nonetheless, for boats that happen to be in the vicinity, it is certainly worth a quick dive just to have a look. You'll find a large living reef that includes many varieties of hard coral, plus lots of leathery soft coral. Most coral growth is fairly low profile, and the huge, ancient bommies found at the other Banks are noticeably lacking. While the scenery is less than spectacular, fish life is plentiful, with a good representation of most reef species.

MARK STRICKLAND

Diver approaches Roe Bank's castle-like fossil coral bommie.

Shark Watching

Sharks are perhaps the most misunderstood of marine animals. Often portrayed as blood-thirsty, evil killers, in reality sharks should be far more afraid of humans than vice versa. While people routinely kill sharks for pleasure and profit, shark aggression toward humans is rare, and unprovoked attacks on divers are almost unheard of. Fortunately, attitudes toward sharks are slowly changing. At least among divers, fear and loathing has largely been replaced by curiosity about these magnificent predators. Many divers even go out of their way to dive with sharks.

To observe sharks at close range usually requires luring the animals with bait. The popularity of "shark attraction" programs attests to the excitement and appeal of such dives. Whether it is a good idea to offer food to sharks or other marine life, however, is the subject of much debate.

Feeding marine animals certainly alters their natural behavior. Though it allows closer observation of otherwise shy species, it typically causes them to lose their fear of humans, in some cases resulting in aggressive behavior. While most shark attraction programs have excellent safety records, dangerous shark behavior may be encouraged by such activities.

Although several species of sharks are found throughout Thailand's diving areas, perhaps the best place to observe these animals is Silvertip Bank. One of the first things divers notice about the silvertip sharks, aside from their obvious power and beauty, is that they are not exactly shy. Frequently, these large predators swim right up to divers, perhaps circle a time or two, then meander on their way down the reef. On other occasions, they may stick around for an entire dive, mostly patrolling in the distance, but periodically moving in for a closer look. Part of this is natural behavior; silvertips are known to be rather bold and curious sharks. However, these animals have also been influenced by years of feeding by dive operators.

Nowadays, even when food is not offered, the silvertips at the Banks tend to approach divers regularly and closely, providing great opportunities for observation and photography. Accordingly, most boats that visit the Banks do not feed the sharks, since it no longer seems necessary.

The debate over the wisdom of attracting sharks is not likely to be settled anytime soon. One thing is certain: Shark feeding is not something that should be attempted by non-professionals—do not be tempted to try it yourself! In the meantime, if you do see a shark, remember to savor the experience. Those of us who get to see these magnificent, threatened predators in their natural environment are indeed privileged.

MARK STRICKLAND

The powerful and beautiful silvertip sharks are not shy.

Andaman Islands

Midway between Thailand and India, the peaks of a submerged mountain range rise up out of the Andaman Sea. The hundreds of resulting islands constitute the Andaman and Nicobar island chains, which consist of a 1,000km long arc (over 620 miles long) from Sumatra in the south extending northward to the Bay of Bengal.

The island chain became a union territory of the Republic of India in 1956. Only since 1993 has India allowed limited tourism development in the Andaman Islands. The Nicobar Islands remain closed to outsiders, and this scenario is unlikely to change anytime soon. Port Blair is the capital, the main port and houses most of the islands' population. It is the only official port of entry to the islands—its small airport receives flights from Madras and Calcutta, India, and all boats (including live-aboards) check in at Port Blair before going anywhere in the region.

Since the Andaman Islands were first opened to tourism, they have been touted as having some of the world's best diving potential—offshore sites offering crystal-clear water were just waiting to be explored. It wasn't long before up-and-coming sites like **Narcondam Island**, with its colorful walls, volcanic topography and equally explosive fish life, lured divers to this far-flung destination. A few enterprising individuals started dive shops on the islands, and several live-aboard operators began making the trip from Phuket, Thailand, nearly 800km (500 miles) away.

KEVIN DAVIDSON

Bumphead parrotfish are seen singly and in herds throughout the Andaman Islands.

The long trip is worth it, as the region's reefs are home to more than 130 coral species. The strong currents throughout much of the region provide nutrient-rich waters that support a wide variety of marine life besides the hard and soft corals—from tiny filter feeders like colorful crinoids to sharks, rays and dense schools of fish.

Fish Rock (near Passage Island) is a great dive where you are likely to see grey reef sharks attacking rainbow runners and dogtooth tuna, large eagle rays patrolling the plankton-rich waters, and a host of small reef critters. **North Cinque Island** (south of Port Blair) offers a nice drift dive with great schooling fish action over the rocky terrain. At Barren Island, an active volcano, divers can discover abundant fish life on a deep and dramatic lava-covered wall. You'll have a very good chance of seeing mantas at the shallow bay on the northeast side of **Passage Island** and may cross paths with a dugong (especially around Little Andaman, Ross and Havelock islands) or saltwater crocodile.

The same conditions that bring divers to the region also attract fishers from India, Thailand, Myanmar and from as far away as Indonesia. Though it is strictly illegal, evidence of dynamite fishing can be found throughout the Andaman Islands (as it is in many parts of Southeast Asia), and damage is extensive on some of the nearshore reefs. The Indian government is making great strides to prevent illegal fishing and promote conservation of the region's resources. Despite the damage, the region's fish life and dramatic underwater scenery remains incredible.

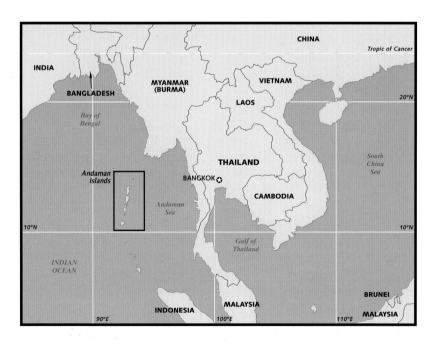

Western Gulf Dive Sites

Palm-lined beaches add to Ko Samui's popularity.

The long and narrow Gulf of Thailand has two main dive regions: the Western Gulf (encompassing the East Coast of the Thai-Malay Peninsula from the Malaysian border north to Chumphon) and the Eastern Gulf (from Pattaya east to the Cambodian border).

The world-renowned Western Gulf islands of Ko Tao and Ko Nang Yuan offer the gulf's best diving and possess a unique diving-oriented atmosphere found nowhere else in Thailand. Ko Samui and Ko Pha-Ngan are also popular vacation destinations, and although the nearby dive sites are only mediocre, these charming tropical islands are still popular with divers as jumping-off points for Ko Tao. Chumphon, the nearest city on the mainland, also has some fair local diving, but is chiefly a transportation hub for those on their way to Ko Tao and Ko Nang Yuan. Learning to dive is an extremely popular activity throughout the region, and for most dive centers, teaching is the bulk of their business.

Most Western Gulf sites can be accessed by half-day or full-day boat trips offered by diving services in Ko Tao, Ko Nang Yuan and Ko Samui. A few Ko Samui shops offer trips to Sail Rock with an overnight stay on Ko Tao, but generally, live-aboards don't operate in this region. Occasionally, boats journey south to the remote islands Ko Kra and Ko Losin, but if you are interested in diving these

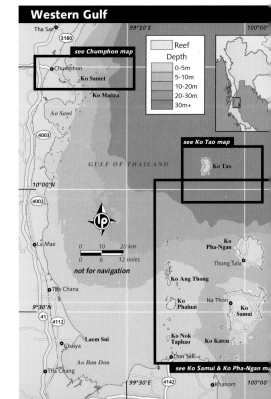

Off the Beaten Track: Ko Kra & Ko Losin

Until recently, diving in the Gulf of Thailand was confined mainly to Pattaya, Ko Samui and Ko Tao. However, a few forward-looking operators are opening up new areas in the gulf by offering live-aboard trips to remote sites like Ko Kra and Ko Losin. Ko Kra is about 60km (35 miles) off of the province of Nakorn Si Thammarat, and Ko Losin lies about 90km (55 miles) from the town of Narathiwat, on the Thai-Malay border. For those who love to get off the beaten track, these sites may be just what you're looking for.

Large animals frequent the two dive areas. You may see several shark species (including whale sharks). Mantas are seen regularly in both areas, probably due to the low number of divers rather than environmental factors. Hard corals abound, as well as barrel sponges, sea whips, plate corals and a few soft corals. Visibility, especially at Ko Losin, is generally better than in other areas of the gulf.

Some Ko Samui dive shops are talking about making trips here with schedules based on demand. Live-aboards are sometimes stationed in Nakorn Si Thammartat and in Narathiwat from May to September (the region's prime dive season). You can also charter a boat to Ko Kra and Ko Losin. Because these sites take a little extra effort to reach, they will probably remain uncrowded for many years to come.

MARK STRICKLAND

far-flung sites, a private charter out of Narathiwat or Nakhon Si Thammarat may be a better way to get there.

Ko Samui & Ko Pha-Ngan

Ko Samui and Ko Pha-Ngan's tourist allure began more than 25 years ago. Backpackers seeking tropical paradise "discovered" these two small islands, which quickly gained fame as the Southeast Asian traveler's paradise—a place where locals were friendly and unpretentious, life was simple and inexpensive and the authorities were mellow and amiable. Those early travelers would no doubt say that "progress" has made the islands unrecognizable, but most would agree that—despite the airport, large resorts and infrastructure improvements like roads, telephones and internet access—the area's charm remains largely intact.

Ko Samui has become one of Southeast Asia's main dive-training centers. Most instruction occurs in the shallow waters of Chaweng Beach, Coral Cove or one of the other secluded little bays or beaches that decorate the island. These days, most if not all Ko Samui dive centers also offer training and recreational diving trips to Ko Tao.

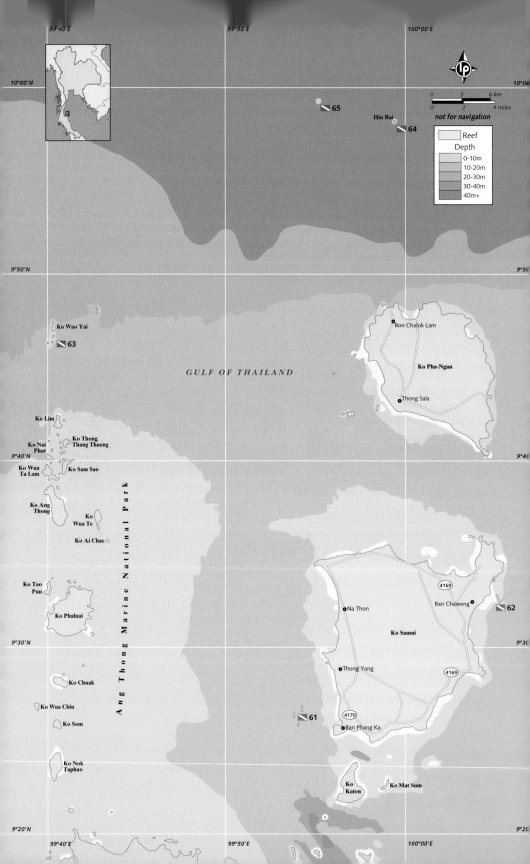

99°40'E   99°50'E   100°00'E

10°00'N   10°00'

65

Hin Bai

64

0   3   6 km
0   2   4 miles

not for navigation

Reef
Depth

0-10m
10-20m
20-30m
30-40m
40m+

9°50'N   9°50

Bon Chalok Lam

Ko Wao Yai

63

GULF OF THAILAND

Ko Pha-Ngan

Thong Sala

Ko Lim

Ko Thong
Thang Thaeng

Ko Nai
Phut

9°40'N

Ko Wua
Ta Lam   Ko Sam Sao   9°40

Ko Ang
Thong

Ko
Wua Te

Ko Ai Chae

4169

Ban Chaweng

62

Ko Tao
Pun

Na Thon

Ko Phaluai

Ko Samui

9°30'N   9°30

Thong Yang

4169

Ko Chuak

61

4170

Ko Wua Chiu

Ban Phang Ka

Ko Som

A n g   T h o n g   M a r i n e   N a t i o n a l   P a r k

Ko Nok
Taphao

Ko
Katen   Ko Mat Sum

9°20'N

99°40'E   99°50'E   100°00'E   9°20

Ko Pha-Ngan, the small island just north of Ko Samui, also has diving centers, and has become very popular as a learning center as well, though it has never really taken off as a diver's destination. It is a place for long-term travelers interested in starry nights, lazy beach days and solving (or avoiding) the world's problems through deep conversation and an occasional mind-altering substance.

Ko Samui and Ko Pha-Ngan have two main dive areas. Sail Rock (also called Hin Bai), to the north, is dived daily from February to September. During the rest of the year, the Ang Thong Marine National Park, northwest of Ko Samui, is the choice spot. Both dive areas are interesting, and though informed divers wouldn't take a dedicated dive vacation to Ko Samui or Ko Pha-Ngan, most will enjoy a few dives in the area. Most dedicated divers visit Ko Tao, to the north, or hop over to Andaman Sea dive sites.

Ko Samui and Ko Pha-Ngan Dive Sites

	Good Snorkeling	Novice	Intermediate	Advanced
61 Five Islands	●	●		
62 Ao Chaweng	●	●		
63 Ang Thong Marine National Park	●	●		
64 Sail Rock (Hin Bai)	●		●	
65 Samran Pinnacle			●	

61 Five Islands

Bird nests are collected from the rocky precipices of this island group for the namesake soup favored by the Chinese. These same high rocks protect the dive site from strong northeast monsoon winds. If bad weather strikes during your Ko Samui stay or if you are limited in the amount of time you have, you'll undoubtedly enjoy the marine life here. It's one of those "better to get wet than stay dry" kind of dives.

Five Islands is used for dive training as well as by more-advanced divers. Although visibility is extremely limited

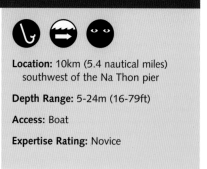

Location: 10km (5.4 nautical miles) southwest of the Na Thon pier

Depth Range: 5-24m (16-79ft)

Access: Boat

Expertise Rating: Novice

due to freshwater runoff, there are a few nice things to see here, such as sea fans and sea anemones, as well as the usual assortment of tropical fish.

White Gold

In several parts of Thailand, small swiftlets (*Collocalia esculenta*) build their nests high up in the marine karst (limestone caves and cliffs) along the Thai-Malay peninsula. Agile collectors make offerings to the cavern spirits before ascending vine-and-bamboo scaffolding to collect the nests—one misstep can lead to a precipitous fall. What makes it worth such risk? Known as "white gold," premium teacup-size nests sell for US$2,000 per kilo.

The nests are made from the birds' saliva, which hardens when exposed to air. The Chinese highly value the bird secretions, believing them to be a medicinal food that imparts vigor. The nests are cooked in chicken broth to make the gourmet food item called "bird's nest soup," in which the nests soften and separate to look like bean thread noodles.

62 Ao Chaweng

Just off the beach from Chaweng Garden restaurant, Ao Chaweng is really the only place for a decent shore dive on Ko Samui. It's a popular site, dived mostly in the summer during the southwest monsoon. The area is serviced by the many dive shops on the beach.

Though the site doesn't have the greatest visibility, it is used for instruction and checkout dives. If you have never seen tropical marine life, it's a nice place to get your sea legs and get an idea of what

Location: East coast of Ko Samui

Depth Range: 0-7m (0-23ft)

Access: Shore or boat

Expertise Rating: Novice

awaits you at the better sites in the region. It's also a nice area to jump into the water with a mask and snorkel on a clear day.

From May to October, the seas here are flat calm, making access very easy from the beach in front of the restaurant. It's a five-minute swim to the reef, which runs parallel to shore for the most part. Most of the reef is quite shallow, with an average depth of about 5m, but often it is even shallower. Here you'll see an assortment of typical reef creatures including parrotfish, groupers, wrasse and scorpionfish, as well as several varieties of hard corals and sponges. Currents are normally not a problem, but it pays to check with a local shop for conditions.

ASHLEY BOYD

Chaweng Beach is a popular shore dive.

63 Ang Thong Marine National Park

The Ang Thong (Golden Urn) Marine National Park is a beautiful archipelago of more than 40 islets. The area, with its limestone pinnacles reaching toward the sky, looks strikingly like Ko Phi Phi. It is the only national park (marine or otherwise) in this part of Thailand, and as there are no buildings or people residing here, it has maintained much of its pristine condition. The park itself encompasses 18 sq km of islands and 84 sq km of marine environment.

Location: 18km (9.7 nautical miles) west of Ko Samui

Depth Range: 0-30m (0-100ft)

Access: Boat

Expertise Rating: Novice

Dive operators run daytrips to this area year-round, and it is an especially good option when the winds are too strong to go to Sail Rock (normally from October to March). Dive sites are less challenging here than at Sail Rock. In recent years it's been a popular place for instruction, and it is not as crowded as Ko Tao or other dive areas frequented by the operators.

Ko Wao and **Hin Yipoon** (meaning Japanese Rock) are the most popular areas for scuba diving and are notable for their shallow caves and colorful soft corals. **Ko Yipoon Noi** and **Ko Yipoon Yai**, at the northernmost point of the marine park, offer the best diving conditions and have a maximum depth of 30m.

Divers see lots of sea snakes, turtles, big snappers, giant barracuda, huge schools of fusiliers and, quite often, what are thought to be dwarf minke whales. Ko Yipoon Noi has some great caves and archways and some of the best untouched coral in the area. While visibility is often poor, the snorkeling and shallow diving, as well as the striking topside scenery, make for an enjoyable outing.

MARK STRICKLAND

The distinctive beak of the hawksbill turtle earned the species its name.

64 Sail Rock (Hin Bai)

Usually dived from February to September, Sail Rock is the preferred daytrip from Ko Samui, since it offers the most exciting diving. You have a better chance of seeing sharks and other large animals here than at other gulf dive sites. Sail Rock's steep above-water topography continues below, dropping sometimes vertically to about 33m.

Begin the dive by exploring the rock clusters at the island's base. They are covered in beautiful *Tubastrea micrantha*, a dark-green hard coral that blooms with green or bright-yellow polyps when it feeds. Black-coral trees with either lime-green or reddish-brown polyps also grow out of the nooks and crannies.

Toward the end of the dive, look for Sail Rock's most famous feature, an

Location: About 32km (17 nautical miles) north of Ko Samui

Depth Range: 0-33m (0-108ft)

Access: Boat

Expertise Rating: Intermediate

underwater chimney with an entrance at 19m on the island's northwest side. Two divers can enter at a time. The cavern continues in for about 2m before bending toward the surface. At 12m you'll spot a hole that opens up to the side and is often guarded by scorpionfish. Although it is a tight squeeze, you can swim to open water through this hole—as long as a scorpionfish sentry is not present—or continue up the chimney, which opens at about 5m. You'll exit the hole to find yourself surrounded by a carpet of anemones and pink anemonefish. Blue-ringed angelfish, parrotfish, batfish and clouds of fusiliers are common.

Black coral and fusiliers at Sail Rock.

65 Samran Pinnacle

This series of underwater pinnacles is dived from Ko Tao, Ko Pha-Ngan and Ko Samui, often in combination with Sail Rock. Although it can be an excellent dive, the reeftop is quite deep, so it's best to descend to 15 or 20m right away to make the most of your bottom time. Fast-running currents can be a problem here, and it's easy to be pushed off course while

Location: 19km (10 nautical miles) north of Ko Pha-Ngan

Depth Range: 15-33m (50-108ft)

Access: Boat

Expertise Rating: Intermediate

descending: It is best to jump in up-current and drift to the dive site. A change of currents can turn this dive into an advanced site, so be cautious and listen to the dive guide before entering the water.

This dive is usually done during the calm summer months. Visibility varies dramatically (as at other dive sites in the area) and is often less than 8m. On a good day, however, visibility can reach up to 30m. Jacks, barracuda, barred mackerel and red snappers are abundant. Despite the efforts of the local dive community to keep it clean, the rock is often covered with lost fishing nets. However, the dive is beautiful, and you'll see fewer divers here than at many of the other sites in the region.

Ko Tao

The sleepy islands of Ko Tao (Turtle Island) and tiny Ko Nang Yuan are about 65km (40 miles) north of Ko Samui and southeast of the coastal town Chumphon. Historically, the major source of income for the islanders was coconut harvesting and light fishing. But since 1990 this area has exploded as a dive destination, and tourism has become the largest source of income. These days there are a number of backpacker-style bungalows, one or two up-market resorts and more than 20 dive centers offering certification classes and scuba and snorkeling trips to the surrounding reefs and pinnacles. Most of the dive centers and bungalows are located on Sairee Beach, on the west side of the island.

An idyllic tropical paradise, Ko Tao attracts divers on lengthy stays in Thailand—many backpackers and other long-term vacationers travel to the island and end up spending months here. The relaxed lifestyle, rustic tropical accommodations, camaraderie between divers and, of course, interesting scuba diving bring visitors back time and time again.

One of the best things about diving around these two small granitic islands is that the dive sites, unlike Phuket's and Ko Samui's, are only minutes away. Including Ko Nang Yuan (which is just a short hop from Ko Tao), there

ASHLEY BOYD

A sunset seen from Mae Haad, Ko Tao.

are more than 25 charted dives sites in the area. Sites range from deep-water pinnacles to shallow coral gardens to rocky points complete with swim-throughs. Although water clarity is sometimes limited, visibility frequently rivals that of the Andaman Sea—30m or more. Again, this may not be typical, but when the water is like this, the diving is truly world-class.

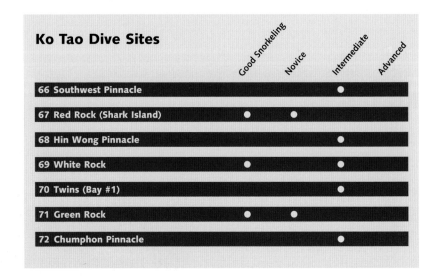

Ko Tao Dive Sites

	Good Snorkeling	Novice	Intermediate	Advanced
66 Southwest Pinnacle				●
67 Red Rock (Shark Island)	●	●		
68 Hin Wong Pinnacle			●	
69 White Rock		●	●	
70 Twins (Bay #1)			●	
71 Green Rock		●	●	
72 Chumphon Pinnacle			●	

Ko Tao

66 Southwest Pinnacle

Southwest Pinnacle, one of the more colorful reefs in the area, is understandably one of the region's better and most popular dives. With soft-coral color rivaling that of corals in the Andaman Sea, it can be one of the better places for wide-angle photography. Visibility, as in most places in the gulf, varies dramatically and changes often. Be careful of the currents here, as they too can change rapidly and catch an inexperienced diver unawares.

The dive site is made up of three pinnacles that form walls and canyons, providing for several interesting dives at one site. Generally, divers enter up-current and drift along the reef, hiding from the current behind each pinnacle. As the dive site is well offshore and in the open, the potential for seeing large schools of pelagic fish such as tunas and jacks is better here than in other places. Bannerfish, butterflyfish, scrawled filefish, masked porcupinefish and groupers may all be seen.

Location: 7km (4 nautical miles) southwest of Ko Tao

Depth Range: 6-33m (20-108ft)

Access: Boat

Expertise Rating: Intermediate

ASHLEY BOYD

Wiebel's butterflyfish near soft coral and black corals.

67 Red Rock (Shark Island)

This site, formed by two large rocky outcroppings that rise above the surface, has some of the best soft corals in the gulf and is popular with divers of all ability levels. Dive operators on Ao Chalok Ban Khao (at the southern end of Ko Tao) frequent this site. Divemasters choose which side to enter from based on your experience level and the prevailing currents.

The shallower part of the dive is at the northeast end, where depths vary from 2 to 6m. This sloping reef structure is acces-

Location: 1km (.5 nautical miles) southeast of Ko Tao

Depth Range: 0-24m (0-79ft)

Access: Boat

Expertise Rating: Novice

sible to divers and snorkelers. Divers can go deeper at the southeast portion of the site, where more-mature and better-formed large coral heads grow.

White-eyed morays, blue-spotted fantail rays, porcupinefish, pufferfish and a variety of other reef fish populate the shallow coral garden. You may see whale sharks, leopard sharks, reef sharks and other pelagics on the deeper side. Lucky divers may spot hawksbill and green turtles, titan triggerfish and sea snakes here.

White-eyed morays peek from their shared crevice.

68　Hin Wong Pinnacle

Another dive with good soft corals but often-limited visibility, Hin Wong Pinnacle lies on the exposed northeastern part of Ko Tao. Like many dive sites with limited visibility, it is more popular with long-term residents than with visiting divers. It is not dived as often as other places because strong northeast winds make it inaccessible for part of the year, and it's farther away than many other popular sites.

The dive site consists of a big granite boulder covered with fire coral. You'll find lacy sea fans and curly wire coral, as well as soft corals in many hues. The resident hawksbill turtle is not shy of divers as long as they keep their distance.

Location: South of Laem Hin Wong, eastern Ko Tao

Depth Range: 3-30m (10-98ft)

Access: Boat

Expertise Rating: Intermediate

Turtles generally rest in the overhangs and ledges along the boulder (especially at night). Take a peek into these areas and you may be rewarded with a glimpse. You may also find turtles cruising around the reef, especially during the day when they are more active.

69 White Rock

White Rock is popular because the dive site is close to the harbor (Mae Haad) and is on the way back from Chumphon Pinnacle. It is often used as the second dive of the day and is also a popular night dive.

It's an interesting site topographically, with short walls, canyons and lots of nooks and crannies that are home to cleaning shrimps, hermit crabs and small moray eels. It has sea whips, some pretty good soft corals, and the fish life is generally prolific.

White Rock is a popular training site, as it's sheltered from wind and currents during the high season (from February to September).

The rubbley areas around White Rock are also prime nesting grounds for titan triggerfish, an unusually aggressive species of fish, a kind of rottweiler of the sea. Triggerfish are hostile during mating season, and will rigorously defend their nests. One individual was especially noteable for his belligerence. "Trevor the Terrible," though no longer living, didn't seem to like anyone no matter what time of year it was. He would sneak up on

Location: Between Ko Tao and Ko Nang Yuan

Depth Range: 2-22m (6.5-72ft)

Access: Boat

Expertise Rating: Novice

divers to bite their hair, mask, fins, regulator or anything that happened to be in his way. Witnesses saw Trevor lying in ambush behind a rock, waiting for divers to look away from his hiding place so that he could spring upon them like an insane warrior.

There are numerous places around Ko Tao (as well as other areas of Thailand) where titan triggerfish reside, though most of these animals are not nearly as combative. They can add an element of excitement to the dive, but be careful to steer clear of their nests. Divemasters on Ko Tao assure us that the terrors of triggerfish are easily avoided if you know the reef and don't linger in their territory—a good guide is invaluable.

White Rock's resident triggerfish can be quite a terror but are easily avoided.

70 Twins (Bay #1)

If you're a critter-loving diver, then you'll be very happy with this site just west of Ko Nang Yuan. All the little things on the two groups of rocks found between 10 and 18m make it a great area for macrophotography. You will probably see anemone shrimp, morays, flatworms and pipefish, as well as busy cleaner wrasse.

Many juveniles reside here, including angelfish and sweetlips. Juvenile sweetlips are a rare sight anywhere and have a fascinating way of "dancing" while hiding in

Location: West of Ko Nang Yuan

Depth Range: 10-18m (33-59ft)

Access: Boat

Expertise Rating: Novice

Look for colorful flatworms.

crevices. The fish, normally adorned with dramatic deep-red and white contrasting colors, swings its whole body from side to side very rapidly and never seems to rest. Anemonefish (both saddleback and the common clown) are seen here, as well as groupers and pufferfish. You'll also find healthy star, staghorn and leaf corals.

Twins and the nearby dive sites **Japanese Gardens (Bay #2)** and **Bay #3** are dived interchangeably as training dives for skill exercises and as second dives.

71 Green Rock

Green Rock is a popular dive site due to the dramatic scenery, which many compare favorably with the Similan Islands. The reef is made up of boulders and rock substrate in which overhangs, small caverns and swim-throughs have formed. These holes are easily navigated without any special tools, training or equipment, so divers can enjoy the feeling of cavern diving without the risks or hassles. It's fun to time your swim with the currents and surge so that the water actually pushes you through the holes in the reef.

This is one of the better places to see brightly colored nudibranchs, morays, parrotfish and blue-ringed angelfish. Whitetip reef sharks are seen from time to time, and large groupers and schools

Location: North of Ko Nang Yuan

Depth Range: 4-28m (13-92ft)

Access: Boat

Expertise Rating: Novice

of yellowtail snappers, fusiliers and silversides frequent the deeper end of the site. In one area aptly referred to as "the minefield," scores of yellowmargin morays and titan triggerfish have made nests on the sandy bottom. Both species are known to react defensively if a diver approaches too closely. Retreat slowly if you see one acting agitated.

72 | Chumphon Pinnacle

Chumphon Pinnacle is the most popular dive near Ko Tao, and in good conditions, it can be a world-class dive site. It's best to arrive as early as possible, before it gets too crowded, or dive it later in the afternoon, when few dive boats visit.

Location: About 5km (2.7 nautical miles) northwest of Ko Nang Yuan

Depth Range: 0-33m (0-108ft)

Access: Boat or live-aboard

Expertise Rating: Intermediate

The rock begins at about 15m and falls beyond 30m. Although it is not one of the most colorful dive sites in the gulf, it is one of the better places in the area to see large animals. Whale sharks and huge schools of jacks are sometimes encountered here. Even rarities like baleen whales and broadbill swordfish have been sighted.

Most days you won't be surrounded by large animals (though it happens on occasion), but nearly all divers are content seeing some of Thailand's largest groupers—some almost as big as a diver. Head northwest from the mooring line to the two large rocks that form a canyon.

On the far side of the larger rock, you'll find a ledge where groupers usually hang out. Groupers are curious by nature and will approach divers closely. Though this makes them easy targets for spearfishers, it is fun for divers. They'll watch you with their big eyes, which give them a "personality" usually lacking in other fish species.

Smaller critters, such as colorful sea anemones and their clownfish compan-

Diver examines barrel sponge at Chumphon Pinnacle.

ions, cover a few areas of Chumphon Pinnacle's reef. Batfish are usually present during your safety stop at the shallower part of the pinnacle.

Chumphon

There are a few dive sites just offshore from the sleepy town of Chumphon on the mainland, though the quality of the diving is nowhere near that of Ko Tao or even Ko Samui. However, many travelers pass through on the way to Ko Tao, and there are speedboats leaving from the pier most mornings, and slower boats at night as well. You'll find a couple of hotels and a few dive operators here, but they usually take divers out to Ko Tao for the best diving.

Chumphon Dive Site	Good Snorkeling	Novice	Intermediate	Advanced
73 Ko Lak Ngam			●	

Chumphon

73 Ko Lak Ngam

Above water, Ko Lak Ngam consists of two barren rock pinnacles. Below the surface, you'll find boulders, crevices and miniwalls. This is probably the best site near the city of Chumphon.

The entry is off the southeast face, between the main pinnacle and the small, nearby rocky outcropping, where you simply descend toward the island and head north with the current. Just to the north is a wide gully, which cuts around the outcrop to the western side. Here you'll find a rock wall that bottoms out at about 20m. The wall is covered with

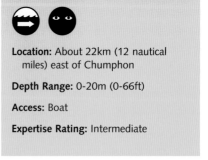

Location: About 22km (12 nautical miles) east of Chumphon

Depth Range: 0-20m (0-66ft)

Access: Boat

Expertise Rating: Intermediate

clams, oysters, patches of encrusting sponges and large barrel sponges. You'll see golden-edge morays and banded sea snakes here, as well as areas of anemones.

Eastern Gulf Dive Sites

Pattaya, Thailand's first resort for foreign tourists, became known as a rest and recuperation destination for American soldiers during the Vietnam War. Thailand's first dive shop opened here during this time, and the servicemen and their visiting families were some of the country's first foreign recreational scuba divers. As the birthplace of Thailand's recreational diving industry, Pattaya has become the center of Eastern Gulf diving and has set examples for diving businesses throughout the country and in other parts of Southeast Asia.

Today's dive shops focus on teaching introductory and Open Water certification courses to new divers. Some dive centers specialize in advanced training programs and technical diving, including deep air, nitrox, trimix (the use of helium) and rebreather training. All dive shops in Pattaya offer daytrips, and some are starting to offer limited live-aboard trips to the Ko Chang area (near the Thai-Cambodian border). Most offer schedules suited to Bangkok residents (both foreign and Thai).

Visitors to the Eastern Gulf will be happy to discover that Thailand's best wreck diving is found here. In fact, Pattaya is the only destination to offer a wide range of wreck dives. Although there are several wrecks scattered around, the three best sites in the area are the Vertical Wreck, the *Petchburi Bremen* and the *Hardeep*.

While still extremely popular with international visitors, the area is also an attractive weekend getaway for Bangkok residents. Although Pattaya is far more densely populated than other tourist areas in Thailand—it resembles Australia's Gold Coast or Hawaii's Waikiki more than Phuket or Ko Samui—its bustle and energy draw many visitors. Its beaches may not be the finest in the gulf, its diving may not be the most extraordinary in Thailand, and its hustle may not make it the most tranquil environment in Southeast Asia. But with a multitude of sporting activities, an unbelievably unfettered nightlife, notable restaurants, world-class hotels and diverse and often low-priced shopping, Pattaya has more to offer than any other Southeast Asian resort. As with Ko Samui in the Western Gulf, Pattaya is not the best place for a dedicated diving vacation, but for scuba students and divers looking for innumerable activities and a busy nightlife, Pattaya may well be the answer.

MARK STRICKLAND

Fishing boats often double as dive boats.

137

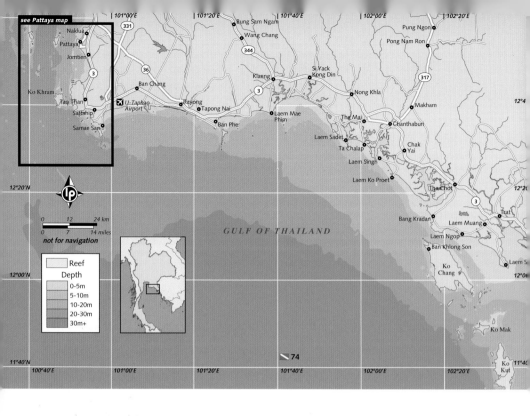

see Pattaya map

GULF OF THAILAND

Reef

Depth
- 0-5m
- 5-10m
- 10-20m
- 20-30m
- 30m+

0   12   24 km
0   7   14 miles
not for navigation

Eastern Gulf Dive Site

Good Snorkeling   Novice   Intermediate   Advanced

74 Vertical Wreck ●

74 Vertical Wreck

One of the most exciting things to happen to Thailand diving in recent years was the sinking and subsequent discovery of the Vertical Wreck, a chemical tanker that supposedly sank in a storm in 1997. Because its offshore location calls for a long boat trip, the Vertical Wreck is usually dived over a weekend (one day of diving and two nights of traveling).

The wreck sits vertically in the water with its bow toward the surface at 5m and its stern on the seafloor at 60m, a

Location: About 120km offshore, between Rayong and Ko Chang

Depth Range: 5-40m+ (15-130ft+)

Access: Boat or live-aboard

Expertise Rating: Advanced

very unusual position for a wreck, to say the least. It is probably sitting this way due to trapped gas in its forward storage compartments—the tanks are made of stainless steel and will not rust, so the gas cannot escape. Though you can't penetrate this area, you can explore the nooks and crannies between the tanks.

Though the crew quarters and the bridge are penetrable, there is not much to see there. Only properly trained and equipped dive teams should attempt penetration, as you must descend to at least 52m to enter. However, you don't need to dive very deep or penetrate the wreck to enjoy this site, which is surrounded by deep-blue, gin-clear water—an unusual phenomenon in the Gulf of Thailand.

The wreck, though not yet encrusted with coral, is teeming with fish life. Batfish school around it, as well as barracuda and large jacks. At the deeper parts of the wreck there are a few Volkswagen-sized jewfish—probably some of the last remaining fish this size in this part of the world.

Continued Exploration: The Ko Chang Area

The Ko Chang area, which is near the Cambodian border, is rich in history and culture. The hilly, jungle-covered islands are strikingly beautiful, and many of the beaches rival those of Thailand's southern islands. Because of political turmoil in Cambodia, very little tourist development has occurred here, but the potential is good, and once things settle down politically, the area will no doubt boom.

Opinions vary widely about just how good the diving is in the Ko Chang area. Some say it is better than diving in the Similans (which is overstating things a bit), and others say it is terrible (which is also incorrect). Clearly, the area needs further exploration, but there are definitely some great diving possibilities. A few dive centers are expanding their services into the area, and live-aboard dive trips are offered on a limited basis.

What excites dive operators most about this region are the underwater pinnacles offshore of Ko Chang, Ko Rang and Ko Kut. Offshore pinnacles and the currents that flow around them provide the nutrient-rich conditions for healthy marine life. Not only are the big animals such as sharks and rays more common, but also the corals and fish life on these pinnacles are far more dense.

As with many of Thailand's pinnacles, operators will need to have onboard GPS navigation systems to find sites consistently and dependably. Once Pattaya's dive operators do more exploration and conduct regular live-aboard trips to the area, we will all hear much more about this destination. It will likely turn into one of the gulf's most popular diving areas.

ASHLEY BOYD

Fishing huts at Ko Chang National Park.

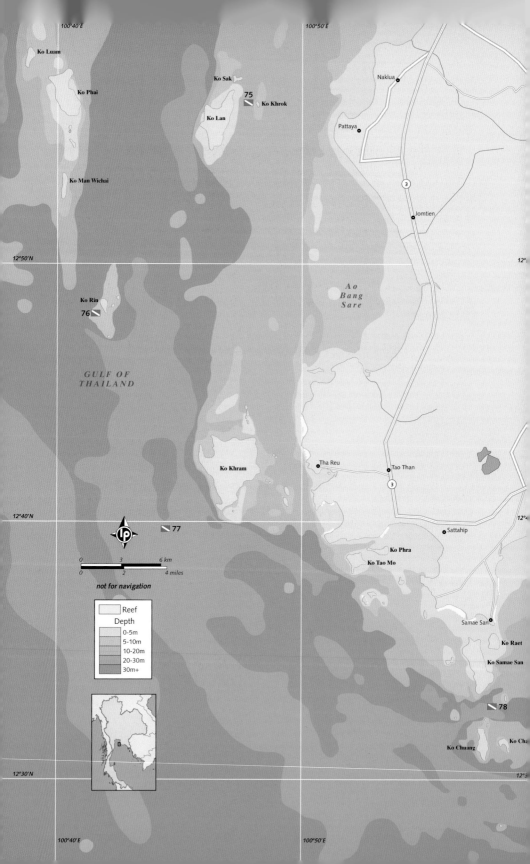

Ko Luam

Ko Phai

Ko Sak

Ko Lan

75 ⬛ Ko Khrok

Ko Man Wichai

Naklua

Pattaya

3

Jomtien

12°50'N

A o
B a n g
S a r e

Ko Rin

76 ⬛

GULF OF
THAILAND

Ko Kham

Tha Reu

Tao Than

3

12°40'N

77 ⬛

Sattahip

Ko Phra

Ko Tao Mo

0   3   6 km
0   2   4 miles

not for navigation

Samae San

Reef
Depth
☐ 0-5m
☐ 5-10m
☐ 10-20m
☐ 20-30m
☐ 30m+

Ko Raet

Ko Samae San

78 ⬛

12°30'N

Ko Chuang

Ko Cha

100°40'E

100°50'E

Pattaya Dive Sites

	Good Snorkeling	Novice	Intermediate	Advanced
75 Ko Khrok	●	●		
76 Ko Rin	●		●	
77 Petchburi Bremen			●	
78 Hardeep			●	

75 Ko Khrok

For an easy coral dive especially suitable for beginners, many operators offer a one-day excursion to the nearby island of Ko Khrok. It is a private island, and no Jet Skis are around to bother divers or snorkelers. This rocky island slopes down into the ocean and is covered with boulder, star and staghorn corals.

Shallow drift dives over the island's coral gardens are quite pleasant, and the added advantage of a short boat ride from Pattaya makes it a popular trip. As it is relatively close to shore, visibility is not often very good, but novice divers will enjoy the beautiful reef fish, including parrotfish, pufferfish, wrasse and anemonefish.

Location: 7km (4 nautical miles) southwest of Pattaya

Depth Range: 0-20m (0-66ft)

Access: Boat

Expertise Rating: Novice

Several Bangkok-based environmental groups began a project to encourage coral growth in the area. The project is funded by both the government and private donors and is an encouraging start toward new environmental policy in the Pattaya area.

76 Ko Rin

Farther offshore than other dive sites in the Pattaya area, Ko Rin offers Pattaya's best coral diving. Despite longer travel times to sites in this area, divers looking for clearer conditions will find the trip worthwhile. Visibility can be excellent, sometimes exceeding 25m, and the underwater profile is more interesting here than at other places in the region. Rocky

Location: 24km (13 nautical miles) southwest of Pattaya

Depth Range: 0-14m (0-46ft)

Access: Boat

Expertise Rating: Intermediate

canyons form swim-throughs that are not only wonderful for divers, but also cause currents to wash around the rocks, which is great for the vast array of marine life that thrives here. Divers will find sea whips and black-coral bushes at around 12m. The fish life is much better than at other areas around Pattaya. Expect to see harelquin sweetips, lionfish, squirrelfish, anemonefish and parrotfish, to name a few. Barrel sponges make the reeftop interesting, and you'll undoubtedly see moray eels and invertebrates such as banded coral shrimp. The area is also good for snorkeling and is very popular with non-divers as a daytrip from Pattaya.

Alabaster sea cucumbers cover barrel sponges.

77 Petchburi Bremen

The *Bremen* is a popular wreck near the village of Sattahip, south of Pattaya. She suffered an engine-room fire in the 1930s and was scuttled, but any other historical details are sketchy.

An excellent deep dive for an advanced course, the wreck rests upright on a sandy bottom at about 25m, and visibility ranges from around 7 to 10m. She has

Location: Between Ko Khram Yai and Sattahip

Depth Range: 19-25m (62-82ft)

Access: Boat

Expertise Rating: Intermediate

been used in demolition exercises by the Royal Thai Navy for years, so she's pretty broken up. This practice has now been stopped, so she is safe to dive on, but the 100m long steel ship's profile continues to naturally deteriorate a little each year.

The ship is damaged to the point where penetration is not really doable, but you can visit what is left of her head, and maybe even lay down in the bathtub. It is also an excellent artificial reef, attracting large schools of yellowtail snappers and barracuda, especially during slack tide.

MARK STRICKLAND

Orange cup corals encrust the *Petchburi Bremen*.

78 *Hardeep*

Location: Between Ko Samae San and Ko Chuang

Depth Range: 21-27m (70-90ft)

Access: Boat

Expertise Rating: Intermediate

The *Hardeep* is considered one of the best nearshore wreck dives in Thailand. Dive shops offer one-day and two-day trips to the site. Located between Ko Samae San and Ko Chuang, the *Hardeep* is a 42m long Indonesian freighter that was sunk by Allied bombing in 1942 and now rests on her side between 21 and 27m.

Today the *Hardeep* is still and tranquil—except for the masses of tropical fish swirling around colonies of fan corals and large barrel sponges that have made this their home. Although visibility is not dependably clear here (averaging about 10m, the same as in the rest of the gulf), the prolific marine life and possibilities for safe wreck penetration make this one of the most inviting dives around. Currents can be strong, so use caution when descending (it's always best to use a descent line) and use the structure of the wreck to shield you from the current.

The superstructure has broken down over the years, but the general shape is still apparent. Parts of the ship, including the funnel and the foremast, lay in the sand surrounding the main area of the wreck. It is possible to safely do a short penetration from the aft hold through the hull to the engine room (the engine was salvaged), and to the boiler room. Avoid bumping any of the beams or deck frames, as corrosion has taken its toll on the integrity of these support parts.

For divers interested in more than shipwrecks, coral diving at Ko Chuang and Ko Samae San (the two islands near the *Hardeep*) can be satisfying as well. Dive centers may offer a coral dive during their trip to the wreck, as both islands have healthy marine life within recreational diving depths. Although larger animals such as sharks and rays are occasionally seen, the big attractions here are the abundance of soft and hard corals and the beautiful, colorful anemones.

ASHLEY BOYD

Wrecks like the *Hardeep* make Pattaya a unique dive destination.

Marine Life

Thailand and its neighboring waters are well within the tropical Indo-Pacific, an area widely considered to contain the highest degree of biodiversity on the planet. A big part of what makes diving so attractive in this part of the world is this great variety of creatures; even the most experienced divers will find plenty of unusual marine life to hold their interest. While space does not permit a comprehensive listing of species here, the following is a sampling of some of the more common marine life, as well as some creatures of special interest. Following that, you will find photos and descriptions of some potentially harmful or dangerous marine life you might encounter in Thai waters.

Common names are used freely but are notoriously inaccurate and inconsistent. The two-part scientific name, usually shown in italics, is more precise. It consists of a genus name followed by a species name. A genus is a group of closely related species that share common features. A species is a recognizable group within a genus whose members are capable of interbreeding. Where the species or genus is unknown, the naming reverts to the next known level: family (F), order (O), class (C) or phylum (Ph).

Common Vertebrates

clown triggerfish
Balistoides conspicillum

ember parrotfish
Scarus rubroviolaceus

freckled hawkfish (juvenile)
Paracirrhites forsteri

bar-cheeked coral trout
Plectropomus maculatus

Russell's snapper
Lutjanus russelli

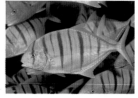
golden trevally (juvenile)
Gnathanodon speciosus

giant squirrelfish
Sargocentron spiniferum

cube boxfish (juvenile)
Ostracion cubicus

orange anemonefish
Amphiprion sandaracinos

golden sergeant
Amblyglyphidodon aureus

longnose filefish
Oxymonacanthus longirostris

red-band basslet
Pseudanthias rubrizonatus

red-tailed butterflyfish
Chaetodon collare

regal angelfish
Pygoplites diacanthus

emperor angelfish
Pomacanthus imperator

lined surgeonfish
Acanthurus lineatus

very-long-nose butterflyfish
Forcipiger longirostris

Indo-Pacific trumpetfish
Aulostomus chinensis

smooth flutemouth
Fistularia commersonii

tawny nurse shark
Nebrius ferrugineus

leopard (also zebra) shark
Stegastoma fasciatum

Common Invertebrates

fine-pored coral
Montipora aequituberculata

mushroom coral
Fungia sp.

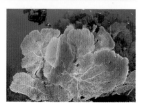

gorgonian fan
Subergorgia mollis

delicate sea whip
Junceella fragilis

soft coral
Dendronephthya sp.

orange cup corals
Tubastraea coccinea

magnificent anemone
Heteractis magnifica

crinoid
Comanthena sp.

cushion star
Culcita novaguineae

jewel-box urchins
Mespilia sp.

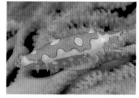

cowrie
Phenacovolva angasi

wentletrap snail
Epitonium billeeanum

burrowing clam
Tridacna crocea

cock's comb oyster
Lopha cristagalli

banded coral shrimp
Stenopus hispidus

mantis shrimp
Odontodactylus scyllarus

alabaster sea cucumber
Synaptula sp.

fried egg nudibranch
Chromodoris annulata

flatworm
Pseudobiceros sp.

pharaoh cuttlefish
Sepia pharaonis

reef octopus
Octopus sp.

Unusual Vertebrates & Invertebrates

giant mantis shrimp
Lysiosquilla sp.

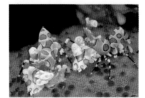

harlequin shrimp
Hymenocera elegans

clown anglerfish
Antennarius maculatus

ribbon eel
Rhinomuraena quaesita

tigertail seahorse
Hippocampus comes

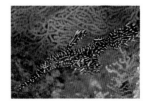

ornate ghost pipefish
Solenostomus paradoxus

Andaman sweetlips
Plectorhinchus sp.

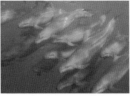

false killer whales
Pseudorca crassidens

whale shark
Rhincodon typus

Hazardous Marine Life

Marine animals almost never attack divers, but many have defensive and offensive weaponry that can be triggered if they feel threatened or annoyed. The ability to recognize hazardous creatures is a valuable asset in avoiding accident and injury. The following are some of the potentially hazardous creatures most commonly found in Thailand.

Jellyfish

Jellyfish sting by releasing the stinging cells called nematocysts contained in their trailing tentacles. As a rule, the longer the tentacles, the more painful the sting. Stings are often irritating and not painful, but should be treated immediately with a decontaminant such as vinegar, rubbing alcohol, baking soda, papain, or dilute household ammonia. Do not flush with fresh water or rub the affected area. Beware that some people may have a stronger reaction than others, in which case you should prepare to resuscitate and seek medical aid. The area may start itching several days after the initial contact; hydrocortisone or antihistamine cream can relieve some of the discomfort.

Sea Bather's Eruption

Often incorrectly called "sea lice," this skin irritation is actually caused by the stings of larval sea anemones or jellyfish, usually on covered areas of the body. Symptoms include itching, burning and red splotches on your skin that can last for several days. Do not flush with fresh water or rub the affected area. To minimize irritation, scrub thoroughly with soap and water and use a decontaminant such as papain or vinegar. Cortisone cream can relieve some of the discomfort.

MARK STRICKLAND

Stinging Hydroid

Looking like small, delicate ferns, hydroids can be brown, yellow, black or white in color, and are common at many coral reefs. While not especially dangerous, these relatives of fire coral can cause significant irritation and burning if they come in contact with bare skin. Treatment is the same as for jellyfish and fire coral stings and sea bather's eruption.

148

Fire Coral

Although often mistaken for stony coral, fire coral is a hydroid colony that secretes a hard, calcareous skeleton. Fire coral grows in many different shapes, often encrusting or taking the form of a variety of reef structures. It is usually identifiable by its tan, mustard or brown color and fingerlike columns with whitish tips. The entire colony is covered by tiny pores and fine, hairlike projections nearly invisible to the unaided eye. Fire coral "stings" by discharging small, specialized cells. Contact causes a burning sensation that lasts for several minutes and may produce red welts on the skin. Treatment is the same as for hydroid and jellyfish stings, and sea bather's eruption.

Fire Sponges

They may be beautiful, but sponges can pack a powerful punch with fine spicules that sting on contact, even after they've washed up on shore. Red sponges often carry the most potent sting, although they are not the only culprits. If you touch a stinging sponge, do not rub the area. Remove visible spicules with tweezers, adhesive tape, rubber cement or a commercial facial peel. Soak in vinegar for 10 to 15 minutes. The pain usually goes away within a day. Hydrocortisone cream can help.

Lionfish & Scorpionfish

At least five species of lionfish are found in Thai waters. Most have distinctive, vertical brown or black bands alternating with narrower pink or white bands. These slow, graceful lionfish extend their feathery pectoral fins as they swim. When threatened or provoked, lionfish inject venom through dorsal spines that can penetrate booties, wetsuits and leather gloves. The wounds can be extremely painful.

spotfin lionfish

Scorpionfish are well-camouflaged creatures with poisonous dorsal spines hidden among their fins. They are often difficult to spot since they typically rest quietly on the bottom or on coral, looking more like rocks. Practice good buoyancy control and watch where you put your hands. Scorpionfish wounds can be excruciating.

To treat a puncture from lionfish or scorpionfish, wash the wound and immerse it in nonscalding hot water for 30-90 minutes. Administer pain medications if necessary. Treat for shock, seek urgent medical aid, and be prepared to administer CPR if necessary.

MARK STRICKLAND

Titan Triggerfish

The largest of all triggerfish, this animal is usually no threat to divers, but will aggressively defend its nest when guarding eggs. Best to give it a wide berth, as it has been known to attack divers for no apparent reason. If bitten, cleanse the wound thoroughly with soap, water and antiseptic, apply antibiotic ointment and monitor for signs of infection.

Moray Eel

Distinguished by their long, thick, snake-like bodies and tapered heads, moray eels come in a variety of colors and patterns. Don't feed them or put your hand in a dark hole—eels have the unfortunate combination of sharp teeth and poor eyesight and will bite if they feel threat-

MARK STRICKLAND

ened. If you are bitten, don't try to pull your hand away suddenly—the teeth slant backward and are extraordinarily sharp. Let the eel release it and then surface slowly. Treat with antiseptics, anti-tetanus and antibiotics; do not tape or otherwise close the wound.

MARK STRICKLAND

Sea Snake

Air-breathing reptiles with a venom that's 20 times stronger than any land snake, sea snakes release venom only when feeding or under extreme distress—so most defensive bites do not contain venom. Sea snakes rarely bite even if they are handled, but avoid touching them. To treat a sea snake bite, use a pressure bandage and immobilize the victim. Try to identify the snake, be prepared to administer CPR and seek urgent medical aid.

Sea Urchin

Sea urchins tend to live in shallow areas near shore and come out of their shelters at night. They vary in coloration and size, with spines ranging from short and blunt to long and needle-sharp. Many urchins have sharp, brittle spines, easily able to penetrate neoprene wetsuits, booties and gloves. Some species also have flowerlike pedicellariae (pincers), which can cause even more pain than the spines. Treat minor punctures by extracting the spines, if possible, and immersing the affected area in nonscalding hot water. If envenomed by pedicellariae, remove these by applying shaving cream or soap and gently shaving the area. More serious injuries require medical attention.

Crown-of-Thorns

This large sea star may have up to 23 arms, although 13 to 18 are more commonly observed. Body coloration can be blue, purple, pink, green or grayish with the spines tinted red or orange. The spines are venomous and can deliver a painful sting even if the animal has been dead for two or three days. Also beware the toxic

pedicellariae between the spines, which can also cause severe pain upon contact. To treat stings, remove any loose spines, soak the affected area in nonscalding hot water for 30-90 minutes and seek medical aid. Neglected wounds may produce serious injury. If you've been stung before, your reaction to another sting may be worse than the first.

Shark

Sharks come in many shapes and sizes. They are most recognizable by their triangular dorsal fin. Though many species are shy, there are occasional attacks.

About 25 species worldwide are considered dangerous to humans. Sharks will generally not attack unless provoked, so don't taunt, tease or feed them. Avoid spearfishing, carrying fish baits or mimicking a wounded fish and your likelihood of being attacked will greatly diminish. Face and

MARK STRICKLAND

quietly watch any shark that is acting aggressively and be prepared to push it away with your camera, knife or tank. If someone is bitten by a shark, stop the bleeding, reassure the patient, treat for shock and seek immediate medical aid.

MARK STRICKLAND

Stingray

Identified by its flattened, diamond-shaped body and wide "wings," stingrays have one or two venomous spines at the base of their tail. Stingrays like shallow waters and tend to rest on silty or sandy bottoms, often burying themselves in the sand. Frequently only the eyes, gill slits and tail are visible. These creatures are harmless unless you sit or step on them. Though injuries are uncommon, wounds are always extremely painful, and often deep and infective. Immerse wound in nonscalding hot water, administer pain medications and seek medical aid. Do not tape or otherwise close the wound.

Cone Shell

Do not touch or pick up cone shells. These mollusks deliver a venomous sting by shooting a tiny poison dart from their funnel-like proboscis. Cone shell stings will cause numbness and can be followed by muscular paralysis, or even respiratory paralysis and heart failure. Immobilize the victim, apply a pressure bandage, be

MARK STRICKLAND

prepared to administer CPR and seek urgent medical aid.

Diving Conservation & Awareness

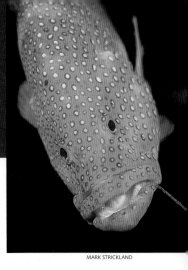

MARK STRICKLAND

Many of Thailand's coral reefs are in very good or even excellent condition, yet environmental threats are just as real here as in other parts of the world. Along nearshore areas, deforestation and overdevelopment cause silty runoff that smothers corals and other delicate marine life. Pollution is also a concern, with sewage from urban areas, toxic chemicals from agriculture and industry, and nonbiodegradable plastic trash all playing a part in threatening reef ecology.

One of the most noticeable threats to the marine environment, however, is the widespread use of destructive fishing methods. With one of the largest fishing fleets in the world, Thailand is among many nations that struggle to balance the livelihood of fishers against the need for conservation. While every fishing technique impacts the environment, some are more harmful than others.

Hook-and-line fishing done on a commercial scale (commonly referred to as longlining) causes great damage throughout Thailand's marine environment. Huge numbers of fish are caught on baited hooks strung out across vast areas. Sharks, which are among the many victims, are especially vulnerable to overfishing, since slow maturation and reproduction rates make it very difficult for their populations to recover. Particularly wasteful is the practice of "finfishing," whereby the sharks' fins, by far the most valuable part, are removed, dried and sold for use in shark-fin soup. As the rest of the animal is worth very little, fishers often discard the body, sometimes still alive, leaving the finless shark to slowly starve to death.

While hook-and-line fishing causes significant damage, bottom-scouring methods like trawling are even more destructive. By dragging large nets across the seafloor, boats using this technique indiscriminately kill everything in their path. Resultant habitat destruction further reduces the chance of many species' recovery.

Another major threat in some areas is blast fishing with dynamite. A cheap and easy way to catch fish, this method is extremely wasteful, since typically only a small percentage of the fish killed are utilized; the majority are left to rot on the bottom. Blast fishing also destroys the coral itself, resulting in a loss of habitat that may take decades to recover. While it is technically illegal, enforcement is difficult, since fishers must be caught virtually in the act to be arrested. On the other hand, the threat of prosecution must be some kind of deterrent, since blast fishing is now rare in many areas where it used to be commonplace.

Coral bleaching—caused by warmer than usual water temperatures—has occurred in several areas around Thailand, but only a few reefs have been significantly impacted. Coral bleaching in this part of the world is only a seasonal problem, and most reefs recover once water temperatures return to normal.

Thailand has made tremendous progress in addressing some of the above concerns, setting an example that other countries would do well to emulate. A good case in point is the extensive use of moorings at dive sites. Ten or fifteen years ago, fishing and diving boats commonly dropped anchor on reefs, thereby causing tremendous damage to delicate corals. In the mid-1980s, a handful of conscientious dive operators started using permanent moorings as an alternative to anchors. As the idea caught on, the government got involved and now works with dive operators to install and maintain moorings throughout the country.

MARK STRICKLAND
Diver installs a mooring to provide an alternative to anchoring on the reef.

Marine Reserves & Regulations

Thailand has done an exemplary job of setting aside natural areas to prevent development and exploitation. The country has more than 150 protected areas, including 79 national parks. Of these, 18 are marine national parks. Fees for visiting marine national parks are extremely modest. At the time of this writing, entry fees are 40 baht per person, plus 300 baht per boat. (In most cases, these fees are included in the price of your dive trip, unless otherwise indicated.)

People living in these areas before they were designated parks were allowed to remain and to develop businesses. As a result, it is not uncommon to find resorts, bungalows, dive shops and other tourism-related businesses on national park lands. As the population and tourism grow, protected areas are increasingly pressured by residential and infrastructure development.

Regulations clearly state that no marine life is to be removed from the national parks. Unfortunately, despite regulations meant to protect these areas, enforcement is often badly lacking. Ironically, even dive boat crews and guests habitually catch and eat the very fish they were just admiring underwater. To do your part, refrain from participating in destructive activities like fishing at dive sites, encourage dive operators to act responsibly, and follow the guidelines listed below in the section on Responsible Diving. If you witness crew or passengers fishing from a dive boat you're on, especially in protected waters, do not hesitate to politely object. Should the dive leader or captain refuse to correct the situation, be sure to let the management know your thoughts. If dive operators hear protests from enough passengers, things may well change for the better; if nobody complains, it is doubtful the situation will improve.

Big Risks for the Biggest Fish

Whale sharks in many parts of the world now face a new threat—commercial fishing. Though few people consider these big fish good to eat, entrepreneurs in countries like Taiwan have created a market for whale shark flesh. In keeping with its bland, tasteless quality it is sold as "tofu shark." Probably due to the novelty of eating such unusual fare, whale shark meat sells for up to US$18 per kilo. At such prices, few fishers can afford to pass up whale sharks, which are slow moving, trusting and, therefore, easy to kill. Since these animals have largely disappeared from Taiwanese waters, seafood companies there are now sponsoring whale shark fisheries in other countries, threatening populations worldwide. In eastern India, more than 1,000 whale sharks were killed in 1998 around just one area! Similar fisheries now operate in the Philippines, Indonesia and, ominously for Thailand, Penang in neighboring Malaysia.

Although the situation does not look very encouraging for whale sharks, there is some cause for optimism. In Thailand, whale sharks are generally revered by fishers and are seldom killed. In fact, there is a campaign underway seeking greater protection for these animals within Thai waters. While this wouldn't guarantee protection, it would at least provide a legal framework to help control trade. Hopefully, as awareness and protection efforts increase, so will the whale sharks' chance for survival as a species. To find out how to help protect these gentle giants, contact the Shark Research Institute at P.O. Box 40, Princeton, NJ 08540, USA; www.sharks.org.

Responsible Diving

Dive sites tend to be located where the reefs and walls display the most beautiful corals and sponges. It only takes a moment—an inadvertently placed hand or knee, or a careless brush or kick with a fin—to destroy this fragile, living part of our delicate ecosystem. By following certain basic guidelines while diving, you can help preserve the ecology and beauty of the reefs:

1. Never drop boat anchors onto a coral reef and take care not to ground boats on coral. Encourage dive operators and regulatory bodies in their efforts to establish permanent moorings at appropriate dive sites.

2. Practice and maintain proper buoyancy control and avoid overweighting. Be aware that buoyancy can change over the period of an extended trip. Initially you may breathe harder and need more weighting; a few days later you may breathe more easily and need less weight. Tip: Use your weight belt and tank position to maintain a horizontal position—raise them to elevate your feet, lower them to elevate your upper body. Also be careful about buoyancy loss: As you go deeper, your wetsuit compresses, as does the air in your BC.

3. Avoid touching living marine organisms with your body and equipment. Coral polyps can be damaged by even the gentlest contact. Never stand on or touch living coral. The use of gloves is no longer recommended: Gloves make it too easy to hold on to the reef. The abrasion caused by gloves may be even more damaging to the reef than your hands are. If you must hold on to the reef, touch only exposed rock or dead coral.

4. Take great care in underwater caves. Spend as little time within them as possible, as your air bubbles can damage fragile organisms. Take turns to inspect the interior of a small cave or under a ledge to lessen the chances of damaging contact.

5. Be conscious of your fins. Even without contact, the surge from heavy fin strokes near the reef can do damage. Avoid full-leg kicks when diving close to the bottom and when leaving a photo scene. When you inadvertently kick something, stop kicking! It seems obvious, but some divers either panic or are totally oblivious when they bump something. When treading water in shallow reef areas, take care not to kick up clouds of sand. Settling sand can smother the delicate reef organisms.

6. Secure any gauges, computer consoles and octopus so they're not dangling—they are like miniature wrecking balls to a reef.

7. When swimming in strong currents, be extra careful about leg kicks and handholds.

8. Photographers should take extra precaution, as cameras and equipment affect buoyancy. Changing f-stops, framing a subject and maintaining position for a photo often conspire to defeat the ideal "no-touch" approach on a reef. When you must use "holdfasts," choose them intelligently (e.g., use one finger only for leverage off an area of dead coral).

9. Resist the temptation to collect or buy coral or shells. Aside from the ecological damage, taking home marine souvenirs depletes the beauty of a site and spoils the enjoyment of others.

10. Ensure that you take home all your trash and any litter you may find as well. Plastics in particular pose a serious threat to marine life.

11. Resist the temptation to feed fish. You may disturb their normal eating habits, encourage aggressive behavior or feed them food that is detrimental to their health.

12. Minimize your disturbance of marine animals. Don't ride on the backs of turtles, manta rays or whale sharks as this can cause them great anxiety. Even if an animal allows you to approach closely, this is not an invitation to touch; keep your hands off the marine life!

Marine Conservation Organizations

Coral reefs and oceans are facing unprecedented environmental pressures, yet there are many reasons to be optimistic about Thailand's marine environment. The last 20 years have seen a tremendous growth of pro-environment interest in Thailand, both within the government and the private sectors. The following groups are actively involved in promoting responsible diving practices, publicizing environmental threats, and lobbying for better policies.

Reef World
www.reef-world.org

WWF - World Wide Fund for Nature
www.wwfthai.ait.ac.th

Wildlife Fund Thailand
www.levantenet.com/wildlifefund

Save Whale Sharks
www.whalesharkthai.com

Listings

Telephone Calls

To call Thailand, dial the international access code of the country you are calling from (11 from the U.S.), + 66 (Thailand's country code), + the city or area code (in parenthesis in these listings), + the six- or seven-digit local number. Note that you must dial a "0" before the city or area code when calling long-distance from within Thailand.

Diving Services

There are countless diving services available throughout Thailand. The following is a broad (but not exhaustive) list of services available regionally. Thai dive shops typically offer a range of rental and retail gear, courses and boat dives (live-aboards and daytrips). Tanks and weights are usually included in the trip price. Many dive centers will even pick you up from where you are staying, except on the smaller islands where there is limited traffic. Most also offer certification and advanced training classes and will accept Open Water referrals from virtually any certification agency. Dive shops accept most major credit cards without a surcharge, but ask before booking.

Shops throughout Thailand are officially required to register with the Tourism Authority of Thailand (TAT), but this registration was not being enforced countrywide at the time of this writing. Registration ensures that the dive centers have paid a bond that covers potential disputes between the dive service and tourist divers. Most of the shops listed here are registered with the TAT and are required to display their certificates in their offices. Many of these shops are also affiliated with PADI, which has its own standards for diving centers. NAUI, BSAC, SSI, IANTD and CMAS have similar programs for dive centers in Thailand, but very few shops are affiliated with these certification agencies. All facilities should prominently display their appropriate affiliations.

Surf Before You Dive

The internet can help make planning a Thailand dive trip fast, easy and inexpensive. Many Thai dive shops have web sites containing dive site descriptions, detailed maps, photographs, layouts of boats, schedules, prices and itineraries—as well as general information on Thailand.

These days, a search engine will produce thousands of references to "diving+thailand." A few other keywords to try are phuket, similan, mergui, tao, samui, pattaya, burma, live-aboard, sailing, whale sharks and, of course, the name of your favorite dive center.

Phuket

Aqarius: The Art of Diving
110/11 Moo 4, Taina Rd., Kata Center,
Tambon Karon, Phuket 83100
☎ (76) 330 432 fax: (76) 330 772
aquarius@loxinfo.co.th
www.aquariusdiving.com
Resort/Hotel Affiliation: Phuket Arcadia
Hotel & Resort
Other Services: live-aboards

Aqua Adventures
54/10 Bangla Rd., Patong, Phuket 83150
☎/fax: (76) 292 088
lp@nicos.net
www.aqua-adventures.net & www.nicos.net
Specialty Courses: Basic and Advanced
Nitrox, Wreck Diver, U/W Video
Other Services: live-aboards

Asian Adventures
237 Rahtutit 200 Year Rd., Patong Beach,
Phuket 83150
☎ (76) 341 799 fax: (76) 341 798

Soi C & N, Patong Beach, Phuket 83150
☎ (76) 292 946 fax: (76) 341 798
info@asian-adventures.com
www.asian-adventures.com
Specialty Courses: Nitrox, IANTD Nitrox,
Advanced Nitrox, Deep Air, Technical Diver,
Cavern Diver, Wreck Diver
Resort/Hotel Affiliation: Adventure Inn
Other Services: live-aboards, courses to
instructor level

Atlantis Adventures – Asia
58/6 Soi Patong Resort, Patong Beach,
Phuket 83150
☎/fax: (76) 344 850
info@phuket-atlantis.com
www.phuket-atlantis.com
Other Services: live-aboards

Calypso Divers
109/17 Taina Rd., Kata Beach, Phuket 83100
☎ (76) 330 869, ☎/fax: (76) 330 544
info@calypsophuket.com
www.calypsophuket.com
Specialty Courses: Nitrox
Resort/Hotel Affiliation: Kata Beach Resort
Other Services: live-aboards

Dive Asia
P.O. Box 70, Kata Beach, Phuket 83100
☎ (76) 330 598 fax: (76) 284 033

36/58-59 Mu 4 Patak Rd., Karon Beach,
Phuket 83100
☎ (76) 396 199

info@diveasia.com
www.diveasia.com
Specialty Courses: Nitrox, Dreager Dolphin
Rebreather, all PADI Specialties
Other Services: live-aboards, courses up to
instructor level

Dive Supply
189 Rat-U-Thit Rd., Patong Beach,
Phuket 83150
☎ (76) 342 511 fax: (76) 342 512
info@divesupply.com
www.divesupply.com
Specialty Courses: IDCs, Rebreather, Nitrox
Other Services: Distributor and retailer,
service and repair work, equipment rental

Elite Sail & Dive
47/6 Vises Rd., M-5, Rawai; Chalong Bay,
P.O. Box 437, Phuket 83130
☎ (76) 280 819 fax: (76) 280 042
info@elite-sail-dive.com
www.elite-sail-dive.com
Other Services: live-aboards, sailing charters

Fantasea Divers
219 Ratutit 200 Yr. Rd., Patong Beach,
Phuket 83150
☎ (76) 340 088, 295 511 fax: (76) 340 309

Marine Center at Laguna Beach Resort,
Laguna Phuket Complex, Bangtao Bay,
Phuket 83110
☎ (76) 324 024 Ext 1703
fax: (76) 324 353 attn: Fantasea Divers
info@fantasea.net
www.fantasea.net
Specialty Courses: U/W photography (live-
aboard cruises only)
Resort/Hotel Affiliation: Laguna Beach Resort
Other Services: live-aboards

High Class Adventure
64/3 Bangla Square, Patong, Phuket 83150
☎/fax: (76) 344 337
info@highclass-adventure.com
www.highclass-adventure.com

Sabai Bungalows - Khao Lak, Takua Pa,
Phang-Nga 82190
☎/fax: (76) 420 143
info@khaolak-diving.com
www.khaolak-diving.com
Resort/Hotel Affiliation: Sabai Bungalows,
The Beach Resort, Palm Beach Resort, Sunset
Resort, Paradise Cabana, Baan Khao Lak,
Baan Ngiang
Other Services: live-aboards

Phuket (continued)

Kon-Tiki Diving School
66/2 Patak Rd., Karon, Phuket 83100
☎ (76) 396 603 or 396 312 fax: (76) 396 313
kontiki@loxinfo.co.th
www.kon-tiki-diving.com

P.O. Box 5 Lam Kean Tai-Muang,
Phang-Nga 82210
☎ (66) 76 420 208 fax: (66) 76 420 120
info@kontiki-khaolak.com
www.kontiki-khaolak.com
Specialty Courses: Shark Diver
Resort/Hotel Affiliation: Khao Lak Laguna,
Bay Front, Similana Resort, Tropicana and
Blue Village Resort, Karon Villa Bungalows,
Phuket Orchid Resort
Other Services: live-aboards, courses up to
instructor level

Ocean Divers
142/6 Thaweewong Rd., Patong Beach,
Kathu, Phuket 83150
☎ (76) 341 273 fax: (76) 341 274
ocean@samart.co.th
www.oceandiversphuket.com
Description of Services: live-aboards

Oceanic Dive Center
P.O. Box 44, Phuket 83100
☎ (76) 333 043 fax: (76) 333 063
thailand@oceanic.se
www.oceanicdivecenter.com
Other Services: live-aboards, courses up to
instructor level

Phuket Scuba Club
5/17 Kata Noi Rd., Moo 2, Kata Beach,
Phuket 83100
☎/fax: (76) 284 026
kevan@loxinfo.co.th
www.phuket-scuba-club.com
Other Services: live-aboards

PIDC Divers
P.O. Box 2, 1/10 Moo 5, Soi Ao Chalong,
Viset Rd., Tambon Rawai, Amphor Muang,
Phuket 83130
☎ (76) 280 644 or 645 fax: (76) 380 219
info@pidcdivers
www.pidcdivers.com
Resort/Hotel Affiliation: Le Jardin, Phuket
Ocean Resort
Other Services: live-aboards, courses up to
instructor level

Santana Diving & Canoeing
222 Taweewong Rd. "Sea Pearl Plaza,"
Patong Beach, Phuket 83150
☎ (76) 294 220 fax: (76) 340 360
lonelyplanet@santanaphuket.com
www.santanaphuket.com

212/12 Soi Kebsap, Patong Beach,
Phuket 83150
☎/fax: (76) 294 017
lonelyplanet@dive-santana-phuket.com
www.dive-santana-phuket.com
Resort/Hotel Affiliation: Sun Hill
Other Services: live-aboards, courses up to
instructor level, canoeing

Scandinavian Divers Liveaboard
177/9-10 Rat-U-Thit 200 Pee Rd., Patong
Beach, Kathu, Phuket 83150
☎ (76) 294 225 fax: (76) 292 408
support@scandinavian-divers.com
www.scandinavian-divers.com
Specialty Courses: Marine Biology, U/W
Photography, Dive Center Management
Resort/Hotel Affiliation: Town in Town 3
Other Services: live-aboards, courses up to
instructor level

Scuba Cat Diving
Patong Beach Rd. (70 meters south of
McDonalds), Patong, Phuket 83150
☎ (76) 293 120 or 121 fax: (76) 293 122
patonglp@scubacat.com
www.scubacat.com

Kata Center, Kata, Phuket 83100
☎/fax: (76) 330 370
katalp@scubacat.com
Specialty Courses: Wreck Diving, Shark ID
Resort/Hotel Affiliation: Thavorn Beach
Village
Other Services: live-aboards, courses up to
instructor level

Scuba Network Services
14/2 Mu 2 Patak Rd., T.Karon A.Muang,
Phuket 83100
☎ (76) 284 217
wiewel@phuket.ksc.co.th
Specialty Courses: Shark Diver, Nitrox
Resort/Hotel Affiliation: Marina Cottage
Other Services: live-aboards, courses up to
instructor level

Phuket (continued)

Scuba Quest
94/11 Moo 3 Kamala, Kathu, Phuket 83120
☎/fax: (76) 271 113
kamala@phuket.ksc.co.th
www.scuba-quest.com
Resort/Hotel Affiliation: Kamala Bay Terraces
Resort, Kamala Beach Hotel, The Club
Other Services: live-aboards

Sea Bees Diving
1/3 Moo 9 Viset Rd., Phuket 83130
☎ (76) 381 765 fax: (76) 280 467
info@sea-bees.com
www.sea-bees.com
Resort/Hotel Affiliation: Thavorn Palm
Beach, Cape Panwa Hotel, Felix Karon
Other Services: live-aboards, courses up to
instructor level

Sea World Dive Team
177/2 Rat U Thit 200 Pee Rd., Patong Beach,
Phuket 83150
☎/fax: (76) 341 595

1 Sawasdirak Rd., Patong Beach,
Phuket 83150
☎/fax: (76) 344 611
seaworld@phuket.ksc.co.th
www.seaworld-phuket.com
Specialty Courses: Nitrox, Rebreather, Photo,
Video
Resort/Hotel Affiliation: Crissey Village
Other Services: live-aboards, courses up to
instructor level

Siam Dive n' Sail
121/9 Patak Rd., Mu 4, Karon, Phuket 83100
☎ (76) 330 967, 330 608 fax: (76) 330 990
info@siamdivers.com
www.siamdivers.com
Specialty Courses: Marine Management
Other Services: live-aboards, courses up to
instructor level

South East Asia Divers
1/16 Moo 9, Viset Rd., Ao Chalong,
Phuket 83130
☎ (76) 281 299 fax: (76) 281 298
info@phuketdive.net
www.phuketdive.net
Specialty Courses: Leopard Shark Awareness

Resort/Hotel Affiliation: Le Meridien Phuket,
Kata Thani Beach Resort
Other Services: live-aboards, courses up to
instructor level, sailing charters

South East Asia Liveaboards
225 Rat-U-Thit Rd., Patong Beach,
Phuket 83150
☎ (76) 340 406, 340 932 fax: (76) 340 586
info@sealiveaboards.com
www.sealiveaboards.com
Other Services: live-aboards, sailing charters,
adventure cruises, kayak safaris

Sunrise Divers
P.O. Box 80, Phuket 83100
☎/fax: (76) 398 040
sunrised@loxinfo.co.th
www.phuketdir.com/sunrisedivers
Other Services: live-aboards

Thai Marine Leisure
The Boat Lagoon, 20/2 Moo 2, Tambon Ko
Kaew, Ampur Muang, Phuket 83200
☎ (76) 239 111, 273 320
fax: (76) 238 974
charters@thaimarine.com
www.thaimarine.com

The Yacht Haven Marina, Laem Maprao
☎ (76) 206 654 fax: (76) 206 653
Specialty Courses: Sailing Instruction
Other Services: Sailing daytrips, Diving
live-aboards

Warm Water Divers - Dive Goods
235 Ratuthit 200 Pee Rd., Patong Beach,
83150, Phuket
☎ (76) 292 201 and 202 fax: (76) 292 203
info@warmwaterdivers.com
www.warmwaterdivers.com

48/1 Diamond Plaza Shopping Center,
104-104/1 Taweewong Rd., Patong Beach
83150, Phuket
☎ (76) 294 150 fax: (76) 294 148
info@thejunk.com
www.thejunk.com
Resort/Hotel Affiliation: Amari Coral Beach
Resort
Other Services: live-aboards

Krabi & Ko Phi Phi

Ao Nang Divers
143 Moo 2, Ao Nang, Krabi 81000
☎ (75) 637 242 to 245 fax: (75) 637 246
info@krabi-seaview.com
www.krabi-seaview.com
Resort/Hotel Affiliation: Krabi Seaview Resort

Barakuda Diving Center
P.O. Box 283, Phi Phi Island, Phuket 83000
☎/fax: (75) 620 698
dive@barakuda.com
www.barakuda.com

H2O Sportz
Palm Beach Travelodge Resort, Phi Phi
Island, Krabi 81000
☎ (76) 270 379 fax: (76) 270 563
h2osport@samart.co.th
www.phuket.com/diving/h2osport.htm
Resort/Hotel Affiliation: Phi Phi Palm Beach
Travelodge Resort

Moskito Diving Center
Phi Phi Island, Ton Sai Bay, Krabi 81000
☎ (1) 229 1361 fax: (76) 217 106
info@moskitodiving.com
www.moskitodiving.com
Specialty Courses: Wreck
Resort/Hotel Affiliation: Phi Phi Princess
Resort
Other Services: live-aboards, courses up to
instructor level

Pee Pee Island Dive Village
89 Satoon Rd., Muang District,
Phuket 83000 (booking office)
☎ (76) 215 014 fax: (76) 214 918
ppisland@phuket.a-net.net.th
Resort/Hotel Affiliation: Phi Phi Island Village

Phi Phi Scuba Diving Center
Ton Sai Village, Phi Phi Island, Krabi 81000
☎ (75) 612 665
info@phiphi-scuba.com
www.phiphi-scuba.com
Specialty Courses: U/W Videographer, Wreck

Trang & Ko Lanta

Koh Lanta Diving Center
81/1-2 Moo 1, Ban Saladan, Ko Lanta,
Krabi 81150
☎ (49) 8158 3236 fax: (49) 8158 3358
christianmietz@t-online.de

The Dive Zone
22 B. 12, Mu 3, Tambon Saladan, Ko Lanta,
Krabi 81150
☎ (75) 620 619 fax: (1) 228 4346
info@thedivezone.com
www.thedivezone.com
Resort/Hotel Affiliation: Phi Phi Island Village

Ko Samui & Ko Pha-Ngan

Big Blue Diving Co. Ltd.
Samui Resotel (Munchies), 17 Moo 3,
Bohphut, Chaweng Beach, Ko Samui,
Surat Thani 84320
☎ (1) 932 6149 ☎/fax: (77) 422 617
samui@bigbluediving.com
www.bigbluediving.com
Specialty Courses: U/W Videographer and
Photographer, Nitrox, Dolphin Rebreather,
DPV (U/W Scooter)
Resort/Hotel Affiliation: Big Blue Resort
(Sairee Beach, Ko Tao), Samui Resotel/
Munchies (Chaweng Beach, Ko Samui)

Buddha View Dive
Thongsala, Ko Pha-Ngan, Surat
Thani 84280

☎ (77) 377 774 fax: (77) 377 910
buddha@samart.co.th
www.buddhaview-diving.com
Resort/Hotel Affiliation: Buddha View Dive
Resort
Other Services: courses to instructor level

Calypso Diving
27/5 Chaweng Rd., Ko Samui, Surat Thani
84320
☎/fax: (77) 422 437
info@calypso-diving.com
www.calypso-diving.com
Resort/Hotel Affiliation: Samui Orchid
Resort & Samui Aquarium, Chumphon
Cabana Resort

Ko Samui & Ko Pha-Ngan (continued)

Discovery Dive Center

Amari Palm Reef Hotel, Chaweng Beach, Ko Samui, Surat Thani 84320
☎ (77) 413 196
simon@discoverydivers.com
www.discoverydivers.com
Resort/Hotel Affiliation: Amari Palm Reef Hotel

The Dive Shop

167/25 Moo 2, Chaweng Beach, Bo Phut, Ko Samui, Surat Thani 84320
☎/fax: (77) 230 232
diveshop@samart.co.th
www.thediveshop.net
Specialty Courses: Nitrox, Rebreather
Resort/Hotel Affiliation: Best Beach Resort
Other Services: Live-aboards, courses up to instructor level

Easy Divers

P.O. Box 61, Ko Samui, Surat Thani 84140
☎ (77) 413 373 fax (77) 413 374

Opposite 'The Deck,' Chaweng Beach Rd., Ko Samui, Surat Thani 84320
☎ (77) 413 373, fax (77) 413 374
easydivers@thaidive.com
www.thaidive.com
Specialty Courses: Cave Diving at Nang Yuan Islands, 'The Beach' Diving Certification at Ang Thong National Marine Park
Resort/Hotel Affiliation: Nang Yuan Island Dive Resort, Paradise Beach Resort, Royal Resort

Pro Divers

125/5 Mu 3 Maret, Lamai Beach, Ko Samui, Surat Thani 84310
☎/fax: (77) 233 399

124/221 Mu 3 Maret, Lamai Beach, Ko Samui, 84310 Surat Thani
☎ (77) 418 435
prodivers@samuinet.com
www.sawadee.com/prodivers
Resort/Hotel Affiliation: Best Beach Resort
Other Services: Live-aboards

SIDS Samui International Diving School

P.O. BOX 40, Chaweng Beach, Ko Samui, Surat Thani 84140
☎ (77) 422 386, 413 050 fax: (77) 231 242
info@planet-scuba.net
www.planet-scuba.net
Specialty Courses: Nitrox, Rebreather Drager, Advanced Mares Rebreather (up to 40m)
Resort/Hotel Affiliation: Central Samui, Central Butterfly Garden, Santiburi Dusit Resort
Other Services: Overnight trips

Unregistered Boats

When shopping for a dive trip, bear in mind that some vessels (typically, but not always, sailboats) offer dive charters without being properly registered with Thai customs or the Tourism Authority of Thailand (TAT). While the consumer is not breaking any laws by using these boats, be aware that such operators have not paid the security deposit required by TAT. This deposit is intended to provide a financial safeguard for consumers in the event that the operator fails to provide the services you paid for. So if there is a dispute with such an operator, you have little recourse. Also, some unregistered operators have acquired a reputation for last minute schedule changes and cancellations. Accordingly, it is wise to look into these details before putting any money down for a dive trip.

Ko Tao, Ko Nang Yuan & Chumphon

Asia Divers
Mae Haad, Ko Tao, Surat Thani 84280
☎ (77) 456 055 fax: (77) 377 910
asiadive@samart.co.th
www.asiadivers.com
Specialty Courses: Videography, Marine
Resource Management
Resort/Hotel Affiliation: AC Resort Sairee
Beach
Other Services: Courses up to instructor level

Ban's Diving Resort
Ko Tao, Surat Thani 84280
☎ (77) 456 061 fax: (77) 377 757
bans@amazingkohtao.com
www.amazingkohtao.com
Specialty Courses: Enriched Air,
Videography, DPV (U/W Scooter)
Other Services: Courses up to instructor level

Big Blue Diving Co., Ltd.
20/1 Moo 1, Ko Tao, Surat Thani 84280
☎ (77) 456 050 fax: (77) 456 045
info@bigbluediving.com
www.bigbluediving.com
Specialty Courses: U/W Videographer and
Photographer, Nitrox, Dolphin Rebreather,
DPV (U/W Scooter)
Resort/Hotel Affiliation: Big Blue Resort

Big Fish Dive Resort
P.O. Box 1, Ko Tao, Surat Thani 84280-102
☎ (77) 456 132
masterinstruct@hotmail.com
www.bigfishresort.com
Specialty Courses: Nitrox, Photography
Resort/Hotel Affiliation: Big Fish Dive Resort

Buddha View Dive Resort
Ko Tao, Surat Thani 84280
☎ (77) 456 074 fax: (77) 456 210
buddha@samart.co.th
www.buddhaview-diving.com
Resort/Hotel Affiliation: Buddha View Dive
Resort
Other Services: Courses to instructor level

Easy Divers
Nang Yuan Island Dive Resort, Surat
Thani 84280
☎/fax: (1) 229 5212

Lomprayah jetty, Mae Haad,
Ko Tao, Surat Thani 84280
☎/fax: (77) 456 010
easydivers@thaidive.com
www.thaidive.com
Specialty Courses: Cave Diving at Nangyuan
Islands, 'The Beach' Diving Certification at
Ang Thong Nation Marine Park
Resort/Hotel Affiliation: Nangyuan Island
Dive Resort

Koh Tao Cottage International Dive Resort
19/1 M3 Chalook Baan Kao, Ko Tao, Surat
Thani 84280
☎ (77) 456 134 fax: (77) 456 133
divektc@samart.co.th
www.samuiwelcome.com/ktc
Resort/Hotel Affiliation: Koh Tao Cottage
Other Services: Courses up to instructor level

Scuba Junction
Haad Sairee, Ko Tao, Surat Thani 84280-102
☎ (77) 456 013 or 164 fax: (77) 456 165
info@scuba-junction.com
www.scuba-junction.com
Specialty Courses: Nitrox (to technical
levels), NASDS, SSI and IANTD Instructor
Courses
Resort/Hotel Affiliation: Sabai Sabai Resort
Other Services: Courses up to instructor level

SIDS Planet Scuba Koh Tao
Ko Tao, Surat Thani 84208
☎ (77) 456 111 fax: (77) 456 110
planet-scuba.kt@planet-scuba.net
www.planet-scuba.net
Specialty Courses: Nitrox, Rebreather
Drager, Advanced Mares Rebreather
(up to 40m)
Resort/Hotel Affiliation: Central Samui,
Central Butterfly Garden, Santiburi Dusit
resort
Other Services: Overnight trips

Taa Toh Lagoon Divers
Ko Tao 84280 Surat Thani
☎ (77) 456 192
taatoh@sawadee.com
www.taatohdivers.com
Specialty Courses: Nitrox
Resort/Hotel Affiliation: Taa Toh Lagoon

Pattaya

AQUArelax Diving Center
183/31 Soi Post Office, Pattaya 20260
☎ (38) 710 900 fax: (38) 710 901
aquarelax@hotmail.com
www.dive-pattaya.com
Specialty Courses: Nitrox
Other Services: Live-aboards

Aqua Adventure
210/1 Mu 9, Soi Buakhao Nongprue,
Banglamung, Pattaya City, Chonburi 20260
☎/fax: (38) 720 657
aquaadv@chonburi.ksc.co.th
Specialty Courses: U/W Photography, Wreck
Other Services: Live-aboards

Elite Divers
287 Moo 5, Soi 12, Naklua, Banglamung,
Pattaya, Chonburi 20260
☎/fax: (38) 367 306
chandler@loxinfo.co.th
www.divingthailand.com
Specialty Courses: Marine Resource
Management, U/W Videography
Other Services: Live-aboards

Ihtiander Co., Ltd.
280/1 Moo.10 Beach Rd., South Pattaya,
Nongprue, Banglamung, Chonburi 20260
☎ (38) 710 208 fax: (38) 422 420
ihtiandr@loxinfo.co.th

127/3 Rat-U-Thit Rd., Paradise Complex,
Patong Beach, Kathu, Phuket 83150
☎/fax: (76) 345 023
Specialty Courses: Meditation diving and
healing
Other Services: Live-aboards

Larry's Dive
597/9, Moo 10, South Pattaya Rd., Pattaya,
Chonburi 20260
☎ (38) 710 998 fax: (38) 710 997

pattaya@larrysdive.com
www.larrysdive.com
Specialty Courses: Dolphin Rebreather
Other Services: Live-aboards

Mermaid's Dive Center
Soi White House, Jomtien Beach,
Chonburi 20260
☎ (38) 232 219 fax: (38) 232 221
mermaids@loxinfo.co.th
www.mermaiddive.com
Specialty Courses: Nitrox, Rebreathers,
Trimix, DPV (U/W Scooter)
Other Services: Overnight trips, courses up
to instructor level

Paradise Scuba Divers
Siam Bayview Hotel, Pattaya Beach road,
Pattaya, Chonburi 20260
☎/fax: (38) 710 567
lscuba@loxinfo.co.th

Thappraya Road 413/136 Moo 12, Jomtien,
Chonburi 20260
☎/fax: (38) 303 333
lscuba@loxinfo.co.th
Resort/Hotel Affiliation: Siam Bayview Hotel
Description of Services: Overnight trips

Scuba Pearl Dive Center
193/165 Mu 10 (Rungland) South Pattaya
Rd., Pattaya, Chonburi 20260
☎ (38) 361 505 fax: (38) 425 645
Amtcom@loxinfo.co.th
Other Services: Live-aboards

Seafari Dive Center
359/2 Soi 5, Pattaya, Chonburi 20260
☎ (38) 429 060 fax: (38) 361 356
seafari@seafari.net
www.seafari.net
Other Services: Overnight trips, courses up
to instructor level

Bangkok

Divelink Thailand
P.O. Box 53, Santisuk Post Office,
Bangkok 10113
☎ (2) 732 7617 fax: (2) 732 7618
Divelinkthailand@hotmail.com
www.geocities.com/TheTropics/2315
Other Services: Live-aboards

Dive Master Co., Ltd.
110/63 Ladprao Soi 18, Ladprao Rd.,
Bangkok 10900
☎ (2) 512 1664, 512 0344 and 0345
fax: (2) 938 4218
divemaster@divemaster.net
www.divemaster.net

Bangkok (continued)

Dive Master Co., Ltd.
16 Asoke Court, Sukhumvit Soi 21,
Sukhumvit Rd., Bangkok 10110
☎ (2) 259 3195 fax: (2) 259 3196
Asoke@divemaster.net
www.divemaster.net
Other Services: Live-aboards

Dive Supply
7/2-3 Sukhumvit Rd. Soi 23,
Bangkok 10110
☎ (2) 661 6088 fax: (2) 661 6089
dsupplybkk@fareast.net.th
Specialty Courses: IDCs, Rebreather, Nitrox
Other Services: Distributor and retailer,
service and repair work, equipment rental

Larry's Dive
8 Sukhumvit Soi 22, Klongtoey,
Bangkok 10110
☎ (2) 663 4563 fax: (2) 663 4561
bangkok@larrysdive.com
www.larrysdive.com
(secondary location in Pattaya)

Specialty Courses: Dolphin Rebreather
Other Services: Live-aboards

Planet Scuba
No 9 Soi 25, Thonglor Sukhumvit 55, Klong
Toey, Bangkok 10110
☎ (2) 712 8188, 712 8407 fax: (2) 712 8748
planet@mozart.inet.co.th
www.wild-planet.co.th
Specialty Courses: Silvertip Shark
Other Services: Live-aboards, courses up to
instructor level

Scandinavian Divers Liveaboard
1207/19, Town in Town 3, Ladprao 94,
Wangtong Lang Bangpai, Bangkok 10301
☎ (2) 559 0230 fax: (2) 559 0230
bangkok@scandinavian-divers.com
www.scandinavian-divers.com
Specialty Courses: Marine Biology, U/W
Photography, Dive Center Management
Other Services: live-aboards, courses up to
instructor level

Live-Aboards

Thailand is home to many live-aboards, most operating in the Andaman Sea. As with dive services, operators change regularly. The list below includes basic information about many of the live-aboards based in the region. It pays to spend some time doing research before booking a live-aboard trip. Boats vary dramatically in terms of comfort and safety features. You can find more information online about each of these boats, and there are countless agents in Thailand and abroad who can help you make an informed choice.

Most live-aboards require advance booking, sometimes many months in advance (especially during holiday periods and from mid-December to mid-April). Full payment is usually required when you book. Many boats will offer discounts to groups or full bookings.

Andaman Sea

Andaman Seafarer
Home port: Phuket
Description: 75ft wood and steel
Accommodations: 3 twin and 2 quad cabins
Destinations: Andaman Sea (Thailand)
Season: November to April
Passengers: 14
Other: A/C, advanced courses, battery
charging tables, photo & video racks

Operated by: PIDC Divers
P.O. Box 2, 1/10 Moo 5, Soi Ao Chalong,
Viset Rd., Tambon Rawai, Amphor Muang,
Phuket 83130
☎ (76) 280 644 or 645 fax: (76) 380 219
info@pidcdivers
www.pidcdivers.com

Andaman Sea (continued)

Anggun
Home port: Phuket
Description: 90ft triple-engine yacht
Accommodations: 2 single, 2 twin-share, 2 double and 1 master state room, all with en suite bath
Destinations: Andaman Sea (Thailand and Myanmar) and Indonesia
Season: Year-round
Passengers: 12
Other: Full A/C, E6 processing, onboard photo/video pro, battery charging station, computer/internet access, reef live survey cam, dive station observing cam, room service, laundry service, canoes, video service, equipment sales and repair
Operated by: Anggun Charter
P.O. Box 191, Karon Post Office, Phuket 83100
☎/fax: (76) 282 379
info@anggun-charter.com
www.anggun-charter.com

Aqua Adventures II
Home port: Phuket
Description: 70ft wood
Accommodations: 2 suites, 3 twin-share, 1 room with 5 beds
Destinations: Andaman Sea (Thailand)
Season: Year-round
Passengers: 12 (15 if private charter)
Other: Nitrox, A/C, battery charging tables, 4 fresh water showers (2 with hot water), onboard photo/video pro
Operated by: Aqua Adventures
54/10 Bangla Rd., Patong, Phuket 83150
☎/fax: (76) 292 088
lp@nicos.net
www.aqua-adventures.net & www.nicos.net

Aqua One
Home port: Phuket
Description: 112ft steel
Accommodations: 2 double and 2 twin master cabins with en suite bath, 5 twin deluxe cabins sharing 3 bath
Destinations: Andaman Sea (Thailand and Myanmar)
Season: October to May
Passengers: 18
Other: A/C, automatic E6 processing, onboard photo pro, satellite phone, dedicated camera/photo room with charging stations, slide projector, 110V/220V outlets

Operated by: Aquasports - Phuket
6 Phang-nga Rd., Phuket 83000
☎ (76) 223 394 (1) 891 6191
aquaone@dive-aquasports.com
www.dive-aquasports.com

Atlantis 2000
Home port: Phuket
Description: 65ft wood
Accommodations: 5 double and 1 quad cabin
Destinations: Andaman Sea (Thailand)
Season: October to July
Passengers: 14
Other: Menu options, A/C, battery charging
Operated by: Atlantis Adventures – Asia
58/6 Soi Patong Resort, Patong Beach, Phuket 83150
☎/fax: (76) 344 850
info@phuket-atlantis.com
www.phuket-atlantis.com

Atlantis 2001
Home port: Phuket
Description: 80ft wood
Accommodations: 8 double or twin cabins
Destinations: Andaman Sea (Thailand)
Season: October to July
Passengers: 16
Other: Menu options, A/C, battery charging
Operated by: Atlantis Adventures – Asia
58/6 Soi Patong Resort, Patong Beach, Phuket 83150
☎/fax: (76) 344 850
info@phuket-atlantis.com
www.phuket-atlantis.com

Crescent
Home port: Phuket
Description: 65ft mono-hull sailing
Accommodations: 1 double, 3 twin (all with en suite bath)
Destinations: Andaman Sea (Myanmar and India)
Season: November to May
Passengers: 8
Other: A/C, Open Water referrals, battery charging tables
Operated by: South East Asia Liveaboards
225 Rat-U-Thit Rd., Patong Beach, Phuket 83150
☎ (76) 340 406, 340 932 fax: (76) 340 586
info@sealiveaboards.com
www.sealiveaboards.com

Andaman Sea (continued)

Daranee
Home port: Phuket
Description: 66ft
Accommodations: 6 twin, 2 standard suite
Destinations: Similan Marine National Park,
Surin Islands
Season: October to May
Passengers: 18
Other: Satellite phone, email and internet,
GPS and Radar, PADI courses
Operated by: Scandinavian Divers Liveaboard
177/9-10 Rat-U-Thit 200 Pee Rd., Patong
Beach, Kathu, Phuket 83150
☎ (76) 294 225 fax: (76) 292 408
support@scandinavian-divers.com
www.scandinavian-divers.com

Discovery
Home port: Phuket
Description: 75ft
Accommodations: 8 twin cabins
Destinations: Andaman Sea (Thailand and
Myanmar)
Season: October to May
Passengers: 16
Other: Open Water referrals, battery charg-
ing tables
Operated by: Santana Diving & Canoeing
222 Taweewong Rd., "Sea Pearl Plaza,"
Patong Beach, Phuket 83150
☎ (76) 294 220 fax: (76) 340 360
lonelyplanet@santanaphuket.com
www.santanaphuket.com

Dive Asia I
Home port: Phuket
Description: 76ft wood
Accommodations: 10 double cabins
Destinations: Andaman Sea (Thailand)
Season: November to May
Passengers: 20
Other: E6 processing, battery charging
station, camera tables, no A/C
Operated by: Dive Asia
P.O. Box 70, Kata Beach, Phuket 83100
☎ (76) 330 598 fax: (76) 284 033
info@diveasia.com
www.diveasia.com

Excalibur
Home port: Phi Phi Island & Phuket
Description: 90ft wood
Accommodations: 8 twin rooms
Destinations: Andaman Sea (Thailand and
Myanmar)
Season: October to May
Passengers: 14
Other: A/C, battery charging, 5
Showers/Toilets
Operated by: Moskito Diving Center
Phi Phi Island, Ton Sai Bay, Krabi 81000
☎ (1) 229 1361 fax: (76) 217 106
info@moskitodiving.com
www.moskitodiving.com

Faah Yai
Home port: Ranong/Phuket
Description: 74ft
Accommodations: 3 doubles, 2 twin
Destinations: Andaman Sea (Thailand and
Myanmar)
Season: November to May
Passengers: 10-12
Other: Large A/C cabins with en suite bath,
three engines
Operated by: Scuba Quest
94/11 Moo 3 Kamala, Kathu, Phuket 83120
☎/fax: (76) 271 113
kamala@phuket.ksc.co.th
www.scuba-quest.com

Ocean Rover
(Commencing operations December 2000)
Home port: Phuket
Description: 100ft steel hull
Accommodations: 6 cabins with queen size
double bed and upper single bunk,
2 twin (bunks)
Destinations: Andaman Sea (Thailand and
Myanmar), Indonesia and Malaysia
Season: Andaman Sea - December to May.
Indonesia/Malaysia - June to October
Passengers: 16
Other: Cruise Director/Photo Pro (Mark
Strickland), E6 processing, charging tables,
underwater photography
Operated by: Fantasea Divers
219 Ratutit 200 Yr. Rd., Patong Beach,
Phuket 83150
☎ (76) 340 088, 295 511 fax: (76) 340 309
info@fantasea.net
www.fantasea.net

Andaman Sea (continued)

Genesis 1
Home port: Phuket
Description: 82ft steel mono-hull
Accommodations: 4 singles, 4 twins
Destinations: Andaman Sea (Thailand and Myanmar)
Season: October to May
Passengers: 12
Other: Cabins feature adjustable A/C and safety box, 2 heads/showers with hot & cold fresh water
Operated by: Genesis Liveaboards
P.O. Box 191, Karon Post Office, Phuket 83100
☎/fax: (76) 280 607
dive@genesis1phuket.com
www.genesis1phuket.com

Jonathan Cruiser
Home port: Phuket
Description: 75ft wood
Accommodations: 3 twin, 12 bunk beds
Destinations: Andaman Sea (Thailand)
Season: October to May
Passengers: 17
Operated by: Scuba Venture Co., Ltd.
33/89 Mu 1, Patak Rd., T. Karon, A. Muang, Phuket 83100
☎ (76) 286 185 fax: (76) 286 184
info@jonathan-cruiser.com
www.jonathan-cruiser.com

Marco Polo
Home port: Phuket
Description: 80ft wood
Accommodations: 1 A/C suite, 2 A/C doubles, and 4 with ventilator and bunk beds
Destinations: Andaman Sea (Thailand)
Season: October to May
Passengers: 14
Other: 3 generators, 3 bathrooms and 4 showers, party deck
Operated by: Sea Bees Diving
1/3 Moo 9 Viset Rd., Phuket 83130
☎ (76) 381 765 fax: (76) 280 467
info@sea-bees.com
www.sea-bees.com

Mare West
Home port: Ranong (transfers from Phuket)
Description: 100ft fiberglass
Accommodations: 8 twin rooms
Destinations: Andaman Sea (Myanmar)
Season: November to May
Passengers: 16
Other: A/C, battery charging, camera tables
Operated by: Dive Asia
P.O. Box 70, Kata Beach, Phuket 83100

☎ (76) 330 598 fax: (76) 284 033
info@diveasia.com
www.diveasia.com

Pelagian
Home port: Phuket & Benoa Harbour (Bali)
Description: 115ft steel
Accommodations: 1 master, 3 deluxe and 2 standard en suite staterooms
Destinations: Andaman Sea (Thailand and Myanmar) and Indonesia
Season: December through May - Thailand and Myanmar. June through December - Indonesia
Passengers: 12
Other: A/C, dedicated photo room, E6 processing, luxury accommodation
Operated by: Dive Asia Pacific (U.S. office)
P.O. Box 22398, Fort Lauderdale, Florida 33335 USA
☎ (954) 229 8022 fax: (954) 351 9740
diveasia@diveres.com
www.dive-asiapacific.com

Sai Mai
Home port: Phuket
Description: 70ft
Accommodations: 4 twin cabins
Destinations: Andaman Sea (Thailand and Myanmar)
Season: October to May
Passengers: 8
Other: Small groups for personalized service, individually controlled A/C cabins, charging units
Operated by: Dive Asia Pacific
c/o M/V Sai Mai Liveaboard Diving Ltd., Part., P.O. Box 244, Phuket 83000
☎/fax: (76) 263 732
info@dive-asiapacific.com
www.dive-asiapacific.com

Scuba Adventure
Home port: Phuket
Description: 80ft wood
Accommodations: 2 en suite cabins, 1 twin-share room, 1 master stateroom
Destinations: Andaman Sea (Thailand)
Season: October to May
Passengers: 8
Other: A/C, onboard photo pro, battery charging tables, U/W video and camera rentals
Operated by: Scuba Cat Diving
Patong Beach Rd., Patong, Phuket
☎ (76) 293 120 or 121 fax: (76) 293 122
patonglp@scubacat.com
www.scubacat.com

Andaman Sea (continued)

Scuba Cat
Home port: Phuket
Description: 105ft steel catamaran
Accommodations: 10 A/C twin cabins
Destinations: Andaman Sea (Thailand)
Season: Similans - November to April.
Racha Yai - June to September.
Passengers: 20
Other: A/C, battery charging tables
(220/110 Volt), Sea Kayaks
Operated by: Scuba Cat Diving
Patong Beach Rd., Patong, Phuket
☎ (76) 293 120 or 121 fax: (76) 293 122
patonglp@scubacat.com
www.scubacat.com

Seraph
Home port: Phuket
Description: 60ft sailing schooner
Accommodations: 2 double, 2 twin
Destinations: Andaman Sea (Thailand
and India)
Season: October to May (sailing charters
year round)
Passengers: 8
Other: A/C, battery charging, huge deck
Operated by: South East Asia Divers
1/16 Moo 9, Viset Rd., Ao Chalong,
Phuket 83130
☎ (76) 281 299 fax: (76) 281 298
info@phuketdive.net
www.phuketdive.net

Short Cut
Home port: Thap Lamu (Khao Lak)
Description: 125ft steel
Accommodations: 4 doubles, 6 quad rooms
Destinations: Andaman Sea (Thailand,
Myanmar and Sumatra)
Season: October to May
Passengers: 32
Other: A/C, E6 processing, on-board digital
video editing including CD-writer, classroom,
battery charging tables
Operated by: High Class Adventure Phuket
64/3 Bangla Square, Patong, Phuket 83150
☎/fax: (76) 344 337
info@highclass-adventure.com
www.highclass-adventure.com

Similan
Home port: Phuket
Description: 70ft wood
Accommodations: 8 double cabins
Destinations: Andaman Sea (Thailand
and India)
Season: October to June
Passengers: 16
Other: A/C, E6 lab, hot showers, Nitrox,
Rebreather, TV, Stereo
Operated by: Sea World Dive Team
177/2 Rat U Thit 200 Pee Rd., Patong
Beach, 83150 Phuket
☎/fax: (76) 341 595
seaworld@phuket.ksc.co.th
www.seaworld-phuket.com

Sor Somboon 2
Home port: Phuket
Description: 80ft wood
Accommodations: 3 triple, 3 single cabins
Destinations: Andaman Sea (Thailand and
Myanmar)
Season: October to May, June to September
Passengers: 12
Other: A/C, battery charging, video, Nitrox
fill station
Operated by: Asian Adventures
237 Rahtutit 200 Year Rd., Patong Beach,
Phuket 83150
☎ (76) 341 799 fax: (76) 341 798
Info@asian-adventures.com
www.asian-adventures.com

Tess
Home port: Phuket
Description: 85ft wooden hull
Accommodations: 10 twin, 2 master state
cabins
Destinations: Andaman Sea (Thailand)
Season: October to May, June to September
Passengers: 20
Other: A/C, Satellite phone, email and
internet services on board, GPS and Radar,
battery charging in every cabin
Operated by: Scandinavian Divers
Liveaboard
177/9-10 Rat-U-Thit 200 Pee Rd., Patong
Beach, Kathu, Phuket 83150
☎ (76) 294 225 fax: (76) 292 408
support@scandinavian-divers.com
www.scandinavian-divers.com

Andaman Sea (continued)

The Junk - June Hong Chian Lee
Home port: Phuket
Description: 110ft Chinese Sailing Junk
Accommodations: 2 doubles, 2 triples and 2 single en suite A/C cabins
Destinations: Andaman Sea (Thailand and Myanmar)
Season: Year-round
Passengers: 18-22
Other: A/C, battery-charging tables, photographer friendly
Operated by: The Dive Inn/Warm Water Divers
235 Ratuthit 200 Pee Rd., Patong Beach, Phuket 83150
☎ (76) 342 186 fax: (76) 342 453
info@thejunk.com
www.thejunk.com

Vilai Samut 9
Home port: Phuket
Description: 85ft wood
Accommodations: 4 quad, 2 triple cabins
Destinations: Andaman Sea (Thailand and Myanmar)

Season: October to May
Passengers: 22
Other: A/C, Video, CD, and battery charging
Operated by: Ocean Divers
142/6 Thaweewong Rd., Patong Beach, Kathu, Phuket 83150
☎ (76) 341 273 fax: (76) 341 274
ocean@samart.co.th
www.oceandiversphuket.com

Wanderlust
Home port: Phuket
Description: 52ft sailing tri-maran
Accommodations: 3 double, 2 singles cabins
Destinations: Andaman Sea (Thailand)
Season: November to May
Passengers: 8
Other: Open Water referrals, battery charging tables.
Operated by: South East Asia Liveaboards
225 Rat-U-Thit Rd, Patong Beach, Phuket 83150
☎ (76) 340 406 or 932 fax: (76) 340 586
info@sealiveaboards.com
www.sealiveaboards.com

Gulf of Thailand

Ariel
Home port: Pattaya City
Description: 65ft
Accommodations: 3 quad cabins and 1 VIP cabin with en suite toilet
Destinations: Gulf of Thailand (south and northeast) and Vertical Wreck
Season: Year-round
Passengers: 18
Other: Onboard photo pro, camera equipment water tub and storage, PADI dive courses, battery charging tables, 4 air banks, 3 showers
Operated by: Aqua Adventure
210/1 Mu 9, Soi Buakhao Nongprue, Banglamung, Pattaya City, Chonburi 20260
☎/fax: (38) 720 657 or (1) 863 2606
aquaadv@chonburi.ksc.co.th

Calypso
Home port: Ko Samui
Description: 56ft wood
Accommodations: 4 en suite cabins
Destinations: Gulf of Thailand

Season: Year-round
Passengers: 12
Operated by: Calypso Diving
27/5 Chaweng Rd., Ko Samui 84320
☎ (77) 422 437 fax: (77) 422 437
info@calypso-diving.com
www.calypso-diving.com

Mermaid's
Home port: Pattaya
Description: 60ft wood
Accommodations: Camping-style on deck
Destinations: Gulf of Thailand (northeast) and Vertical Wreck
Season: Year-round
Passengers: 15
Operated by: Mermaid's Dive Center
Soi White House, Jomtien Beach, Chonburi 20260
mermaids@loxinfo.co.th
www.mermaiddive.com
☎ (38) 232 219 or 220
fax: (38) 232 221

Gulf of Thailand (continued)

Mook-Talay (Sea Pearl)
Home port: Pattaya
Description: 53ft fiberglass
Accommodations: 2 en suite cabins for 8
Destinations: Ko Chang, Vertical Wreck,
Samaesan, Pattaya's islands
Season: Year-round
Passengers: 15 for daytrip, 8 for live-aboard
Other: A/C, Open Water referrals, battery
charging tables
Operated by: Scuba Pearl Dive Center
193/165 Mu 10 (Rungland) South Pattaya
Rd., Pattaya City, Chonburi 20260
☎ (38) 361 505 fax: (38) 425 645
Amtcom@loxinfo.co.th

Oasis
Home port: Ko Samui
Description: 110ft wood
Accommodations: Private bunks in dorm
Destinations: Ko Tao, Ko Kra
Season: January to October
Passengers: 16
Operated by: The Dive Shop
167/25 Moo 2, Chaweng Beach, Bo Phut,
Ko Samui 84140
☎/fax: (77) 230 232
diveshop@samart.co.th
www.thediveshop.net

Tourist Offices

The Tourism Authority of Thailand (TAT), with offices throughout Thailand and the world, provides information about entry requirements, accommodations, activities, attractions, holidays and more. Their comprehensive website (www .tourismthailand.org) can be a great help in planning your trip, and lists the contact information for each of their offices. The main office is in the Le Concorde Building, 202 Ratchadaphisek Road, Huai Khwang, Bangkok 10310, Thailand, ☎ (662) 694 1222 fax: (662) 694 1220 or 1221.

In Bangkok you'll find **TAT Information Counters** at the following locations:

- Arrival Hall Don Muang Airport, Terminal 1. ☎ (662) 523 8972 or 8973
  Open daily 8am to midnight

- Arrival Hall Don Muang Airport, Terminal 2. ☎ (662) 535 2669
  Open daily 8am to midnight

- 4 Ratchadamnoen Nok Ave., Bangkok 10100.
  ☎ (662) 282 9773 through 9776
  Open daily 8:30am to 4:30pm

- 10th floor, Le Concorde Building, 202 Ratchadapisek Rd., Huai Khwang, Bangkok 10310. ☎ (662) 694 1222 ext. 1000 through 1004
  Open weekdays 8:30am to 4:30pm

- Chatuchak Weekend Market, Phahonyothin Rd., Bangkok.
  Open weekends 9am to 5pm

The one-stop, 24-hour **Tourist Service Center** assists tourists with any complaint or emergency, and provides general tourist information. It is located at 4 Ratchadamnoen Nok Avenue, Bangkok, and has a toll-free hotline service ☎ 1155.

Index

dive sites covered in this book appear in **bold** type

Lonely Planet Pisces Books

The **Diving & Snorkeling** guides cover top destinations worldwide. Beautifully illustrated with full-color photos throughout, the series explores the best diving and snorkeling areas and prepares divers for what to expect when they get there. Each site is described in detail, with information on suggested ability levels, depth, visibility and, of course, marine life. There's basic topside information as well for each destination.

Also check out dive guides to:

Australia: Southeast Coast	British Virgin Islands	Monterey Peninsula & Northern California	Seychelles
Bahamas: Family Islands & Grand Bahama	Cocos Island	Pacific Northwest	Southern California
Bahamas: Nassau & New Providence	Curaçao	Puerto Rico	Texas
Bali & the Komodo Region	Dominica	Red Sea	Turks & Caicos
Bermuda	Florida Keys	Roatan & Honduras' Bay Islands	U.S. Virgin Islands
Bonaire	Guam & Yap	Scotland	Vanuatu
	Jamaica		